CONTENTS

D0420250

*F*ABULOUS *D*ESSERTS

Designed for today's faster paced lifestyles, HERSHEY'S FABULOUS DESSERTS is an exciting new cookbook for people who want the quality of homemade desserts but have little time to prepare them.

At Hershey, we know you can buy good ready-made desserts at the grocery store or bakery. But we also know that ready-made doesn't deliver the great taste and personal satisfaction gained from a scratch recipe made with love for family and friends. HERSHEY'S FABULOUS DESSERTS is especially designed for convenience as well as to deliver the quality and satisfaction that are so important in the chocolate desserts you serve.

We live with the same time constraints you do, and we're always looking for kitchen shortcuts that don't sacrifice quality. That's not easy, but we think we've accomplished it in the recipes offered here. Throughout this book we've used the following symbols to emphasize the types of recipes presented:

😀 **SUPERFAST**   **Can be prepared within 5 minutes.**

🥧 **NO BAKE**   **No conventional baking needed.**

🌓 **MAKE AHEAD**   **Avoid last minute preparation.**

🌀 **MICROWAVE**   **Microwave oven used for cooking/baking/melting.**

📦 **CONVENIENCE MIX**   **Starts with a convenience product.**

We hope these symbols make your dessert planning easier and simply more fun.

All the recipes in this book are made with the same fine Hershey's baking products you've known and trusted for generations. We're very excited about this new cookbook, and after you try some of our recipes, we hope you'll be excited too.

CHOCOLATE IS CHOCOLATE...OR IS IT?

Almost everyone loves the flavor of chocolate, but most people don't realize that chocolate comes in a variety of forms. Here's a little background:

Cacao (Cocoa) Beans are the starting point. They are the fruit of the cacao tree, which grows in a very limited climate zone—only 20 degrees north and south of the Equator—and mainly in West Africa and Latin America.

Cacao Nibs are the "meat" of the beans. The beans are cleaned and then roasted at carefully controlled temperatures to bring out their full flavor and aroma. When the outer shells are removed, the nibs are ready to go on to greater things.

Chocolate Liquor is what makes all real chocolate products possible. The nibs are ground by a process that generates enough heat to liquefy the cocoa butter, thus creating the liquor. ("Liquor" here is used in its true sense, that of liquid essence, and has nothing to do with alcohol.)

Cocoa Butter is the vegetable fat that's extracted when the chocolate liquor is "pressed" under high pressure. This butter has a distinctive melting quality that gives chocolate products their unique texture.

Dutch-Process Cocoa Powder is made from chocolate liquor that has been treated with an alkali agent. This makes a darker powder, with a flavor that differs from American-process cocoa.

Unsweetened Chocolate also referred to as bitter, baking or cooking chocolate, is pure chocolate liquor, cooled and molded, usually in blocks.

Semi-Sweet Chocolate is a combination of chocolate liquor with added cocoa butter and sugar. To qualify for this term, the product must contain at least 35% chocolate liquor. Available in bars and more popularly as chips.

Sweet (Dark) Chocolate combines the same ingredients as semi-sweet, but the balance is different. This form must contain at least 15% chocolate liquor and has a higher sugar level.

Milk Chocolate also uses the same ingredients as semi-sweet but with the addition of milk or cream. At least 10% chocolate liquor is required in milk chocolate products.

White Chocolate is known in the chocolate industry as compound chocolate. It isn't really chocolate at all. Most or all of the cocoa butter has been removed and replaced by another vegetable fat, and it contains no chocolate liquor. Available in blocks or as vanilla milk chips.

Chocolate-Flavored is the term applied to food products that derive their flavor from cocoa and/or chocolate liquor but do not contain enough cocoa or chocolate liquor to be considered "true" chocolate. Chocolate-flavored syrups, which combine chocolate liquor or cocoa, sugar, water, salt and sometimes other flavorings, are an example.

Artificial Chocolate is a product of the chemical industry, not chocolate-makers. Such products contain no ingredients derived from the cacao bean.

CAKES

Indulge yourself with any one of these wonderful easy-to-make cakes.

From left to right: Chocolate Sour Cream Cake (recipe page 17), Peanut Butter-Fudge Marble Cake and Devil's Delight Cake (recipes page 6)

Devil's Delight Cake 🄳

1 package (18.25 ounces)
　　devil's food cake mix (with
　　pudding in the mix)
4 eggs
1 cup water
1/2 cup vegetable oil
1 cup chopped nuts
1 cup miniature marshmallows
1 cup HERSHEY'S Semi-Sweet
　　Chocolate Chips
1/2 cup raisins
　　Confectioners' sugar or
　　Chocolate Chip Glaze
　　(recipe follows)

Heat oven to 350°. Grease and
flour 12-cup Bundt pan. In large
mixer bowl combine cake mix,
eggs, water and oil; beat on low
speed just until blended. Increase
speed to medium; beat 2 minutes.
Stir in nuts, marshmallows,
chocolate chips and raisins. Pour
batter into prepared pan. Bake 45
to 50 minutes or until wooden pick
inserted in center comes out
clean. Cool 10 minutes; remove
from pan to wire rack. Cool
completely. Sprinkle confectioners'
sugar over top or drizzle
Chocolate Chip Glaze over top.
　　　　　　　　　　12 to 16 servings

Chocolate Chip Glaze 🄲

In small saucepan combine
2 tablespoons butter or margarine,
2 tablespoons light corn syrup
and 2 tablespoons water. Cook
over low heat, stirring constantly,
until mixture begins to boil.
Remove from heat; add 1 cup
HERSHEY'S Semi-Sweet Chocolate
Chips. Stir until chips are melted
and mixture is smooth. Continue
stirring until glaze is desired
consistency.

　　　　　　　　　　About 1 cup glaze

Peanut Butter-Fudge Marble Cake 🄳

1 package (18.25 or 19.75
　　ounces) fudge marble
　　cake mix
3 eggs
1/3 cup plus 2 tablespoons
　　vegetable oil, divided
Water
1 cup REESE'S Peanut Butter
　　Chips

Heat oven to 350°. Grease and
flour two 8- or 9-inch round baking
pans. Prepare cake batters
according to package directions
using eggs, 1/3 cup oil and water.
In top of double boiler over hot,
not boiling, water melt peanut
butter chips with remaining 2
tablespoons oil, stirring constantly.
OR, in small microwave-safe bowl
place chips and oil. Microwave at
HIGH (100%) 45 seconds; stir. If
necessary, microwave at HIGH
additional 15 seconds or until
melted and smooth when stirred.
Gradually add peanut butter
mixture to vanilla batter, blending
well. Pour peanut butter batter into
prepared pans. Randomly place
spoonfuls of chocolate batter on
top; swirl as directed on package.
Bake 30 to 40 minutes or until
wooden pick inserted in center
comes out clean. Cool 15 minutes;
remove from pans to wire rack.
Cool completely; frost as
desired.　　　　　　*10 to 12 servings*

Microwave Chocolate Cake Ⓝ

1/4 cup HERSHEY'S Cocoa
2/3 cup hot water, divided
3/4 cup plus 2 tablespoons all-purpose flour
1 cup sugar
1/2 teaspoon baking soda
1/4 teaspoon baking powder
1/4 teaspoon salt
1/4 cup plus 2 tablespoons vegetable oil
1 egg
2 teaspoons vanilla extract
Easy Cocoa Frosting (recipe follows)

Grease microwave-safe 7¼ x 2¼-inch or 8 x 1½-inch round baking dish. Line bottom of dish with plastic wrap. In small microwave-safe bowl combine cocoa and 1/3 cup water; microwave at HIGH (100%) 40 to 50 seconds or until very hot and slightly thickened. In medium bowl combine flour, sugar, baking soda, baking powder and salt. Add oil, remaining 1/3 cup hot water, egg, vanilla and chocolate mixture; beat with whisk 40 to 50 strokes or until batter is smooth and well blended. Pour batter into prepared pan. Microwave at HIGH 5 to 6 minutes*, without turning, until cake begins to pull away from sides (some moist spots may remain but will disappear on standing). Let stand 5 minutes; invert onto serving plate. Peel off plastic wrap; cool. Frost with Easy Cocoa Frosting. Garnish as desired.   *About 8 servings*

*Time is for 600-700 watt microwave ovens. Increase baking time for lower wattage ovens.

Easy Cocoa Frosting Ⓔ

3 tablespoons butter or margarine, softened
1/4 cup HERSHEY'S Cocoa
1 1/3 cups confectioners' sugar
2 to 3 tablespoons milk
1/2 teaspoon vanilla extract

In small mixer bowl combine all ingredients; beat to spreading consistency.
     About 1 cup frosting

Marbled Angel Cake ⊙

1 box (14.5 ounces) angel
   food cake mix
1/4 cup HERSHEY'S Cocoa
   Chocolate Glaze (recipe
   follows)

Adjust oven rack to lowest position.
Heat oven to 375°. Prepare cake
batter according to package
directions. Measure 4 cups batter
into separate bowl; gradually fold
cocoa into this batter until well
blended, being careful not to
deflate batter. Alternately pour
vanilla and chocolate batters into
ungreased 10-inch tube pan. Cut
through batter with knife or
spatula to marble batter. Bake 30
to 35 minutes or until top crust is
firm and looks very dry. Do not
underbake. Invert pan on heat-
proof funnel or bottle; cool at least
1 1/2 hours. Carefully run knife
along side of pan to loosen cake.
Place on serving plate; drizzle with
Chocolate Glaze.

12 to 16 servings

Chocolate Glaze 🟤
In small saucepan bring 1/3 cup
sugar and 1/4 cup water to full
boil, stirring until sugar dissolves.
Remove from heat; add 1 cup
HERSHEY'S MINI CHIPS Semi-Sweet
Chocolate. Stir with wire whisk until
chips are melted and mixture is
smooth. Cool to desired
consistency; use immediately.

About 2/3 cup glaze

Chocolate Cake with Crumb Topping

Crumb Topping (recipe
   follows)
1 1/2 cups all-purpose flour
1 cup sugar
1/4 cup HERSHEY'S Cocoa
1 teaspoon baking soda
1/2 teaspoon salt
1 cup water
1/4 cup plus 2 tablespoons
   vegetable oil
1 tablespoon white vinegar
1 teaspoon vanilla extract
Whipped topping or ice
   cream (optional)

Prepare Crumb Topping; set aside.
Heat oven to 350°. Grease and
flour 9-inch square baking pan. In
medium bowl combine flour,
sugar, cocoa, baking soda and
salt. Add water, oil, vinegar and
vanilla; beat with spoon or wire
whisk just until batter is smooth
and ingredients are well blended.
Pour batter into prepared pan.
Sprinkle topping over batter. Bake
35 minutes or until wooden pick
inserted in center comes out
clean. Cool in pan on wire rack.
Serve with whipped topping or ice
cream, if desired.

About 9 servings

Crumb Topping
In small bowl combine 1/2 cup
graham cracker crumbs, 1/4 cup
chopped nuts and 2 tablespoons
melted butter or margarine. Stir in
1/2 cup HERSHEY'S Semi-Sweet
Chocolate Chips.

*Marbled Angel Cake (top) and
Chocolate Cake with Crumb Topping
(bottom)*

*E*asy Peanut Butter-Chakolate Chip Cake 🍫

- 1 package (18.5 ounces) yellow cake mix (with pudding in the mix)
- 4 eggs
- 3/4 cup water
- 1/3 cup vegetable oil
- 1/3 cup creamy peanut butter
- 1 1/2 cups HERSHEY'S Semi-Sweet Chocolate Chips, divided
- 1/4 cup chopped, unsalted peanuts

Heat oven to 350°. Grease and lightly flour 13 × 9 × 2-inch baking pan. Prepare cake batter according to package directions using eggs, water and oil. Blend in peanut butter. Spoon half of batter into prepared pan. Sprinkle 3/4 cup chocolate chips over batter. Gently spread remaining batter over top. Sprinkle remaining 3/4 cup chips and peanuts over batter. Bake 45 minutes or until wooden pick inserted in center comes out clean. Cool in pan on wire rack.   *12 to 15 servings*

*D*ouble Marble Cake 🍫

- 1 package (18.25 or 19.75 ounces) fudge marble cake mix
- 3 eggs
- 1/3 cup vegetable oil
  Water
- 1 cup HERSHEY'S Semi-Sweet Chocolate Chips, divided
- 1 jar (7 ounces) marshmallow creme

Heat oven to 350°. Grease and flour 13 × 9 × 2-inch baking pan. Prepare cake batters according to package directions, using eggs, oil and water. Stir 1/2 cup chocolate chips into chocolate batter. Spoon vanilla and chocolate batters into prepared pan; swirl as directed on package. Bake 33 to 38 minutes or until wooden pick inserted in center comes out clean. Cool in pan on wire rack 5 minutes. Gently spread marshmallow creme over warm cake. In small saucepan over low heat melt remaining 1/2 cup chips; swirl through marshmallow creme. Cool thoroughly.   *12 to 15 servings*

VARIATION
Chocolate Banana Snack Cake: Decrease water to ¹/₂ cup; stir in ¹/₂ cup mashed, ripe banana (1 medium banana) before pouring batter into pan.

Double Chocolate Snack Cake

- 1²/₃ cups all-purpose flour
- 1 cup packed light brown sugar
- ¹/₄ cup HERSHEY'S Cocoa
- 1 teaspoon baking soda
- ¹/₄ teaspoon salt
- 1 cup water
- ¹/₃ cup vegetable oil
- 1 teaspoon white vinegar
- ³/₄ teaspoon vanilla extract
- ¹/₂ cup HERSHEY'S Semi-Sweet Chocolate Chips

Heat oven to 350°. Grease and flour 8-inch square baking pan. In small bowl combine flour, sugar, cocoa, baking soda and salt. Add water, oil, vinegar and vanilla; beat with spoon or wire whisk until smooth. Pour batter into prepared pan. Sprinkle chocolate chips over top. Bake 35 to 40 minutes or until wooden pick inserted in center comes out clean. Cool in pan on wire rack.

6 to 8 servings

Chocolate Raisin Snacking Cake

- ³/₄ cup raisins
- 1 cup water
- 1¹/₄ cups granulated sugar
- ²/₃ cup vegetable oil
- 1 egg, slightly beaten
- 1³/₄ cups all-purpose flour
- ¹/₃ cup HERSHEY'S Cocoa
- 1 teaspoon baking soda
- ¹/₂ teaspoon salt
- ¹/₄ teaspoon ground cinnamon
- ¹/₂ cup chopped nuts
  Confectioners' sugar

Heat oven to 350°. Grease and flour 13 × 9 × 2-inch baking pan. In medium saucepan bring raisins and water to boil; simmer 1 minute. Remove from heat; cool slightly. Stir in granulated sugar and oil. Add egg. Combine flour, cocoa, baking soda, salt and cinnamon; stir into raisin mixture, blending well. Stir in nuts. Pour batter into prepared pan. Bake 25 to 30 minutes or until wooden pick inserted in center comes out clean. Sprinkle confectioners' sugar over warm cake. Cool in pan on wire rack.

12 to 15 servings

Cocoa Oatmeal Cake

1 1/3 cups boiling water
1 cup quick-cooking rolled oats
1/2 cup butter or margarine, softened
1 cup granulated sugar
1 cup packed light brown sugar
2 eggs
1 1/2 cups all-purpose flour
1/2 cup HERSHEY'S Cocoa
1 teaspoon baking powder
1 teaspoon baking soda
1/4 teaspoon ground cinnamon
1 cup finely chopped, peeled apple
1 cup chopped nuts
Vanilla Glaze (recipe follows)

In small bowl pour boiling water over oats; let stand 15 minutes. Heat oven to 350°. Grease and flour 13 x 9 x 2-inch baking pan. In large mixer bowl cream butter, granulated sugar, brown sugar and eggs until light and fluffy. Blend in oat mixture. Combine flour, cocoa, baking powder, baking soda and cinnamon; add to creamed mixture, mixing well. Stir in apple and nuts. Pour batter into prepared pan. Bake 30 to 35 minutes or until wooden pick inserted in center comes out clean. Cool in pan on wire rack; drizzle Vanilla Glaze over top in decorative design.

12 to 15 servings

Vanilla Glaze

1 cup confectioners' sugar
1 tablespoon butter or margarine, softened
1 to 2 tablespoons hot water
1/2 teaspoon vanilla extract

In small bowl beat all ingredients with spoon or wire whisk until smooth.

Chocolate Chip Orange Pound Cake

- ½ cup butter, softened
- 4 ounces (½ of 8-ounce package) cream cheese, softened
- ¾ cup sugar
- 2 eggs
- 1 teaspoon vanilla extract
- ¼ teaspoon grated orange peel
- 1 cup all-purpose flour
- 1 teaspoon baking powder
- 1 cup HERSHEY'S MINI CHIPS Semi-Sweet Chocolate
  Confectioners' sugar

Heat oven to 325°. Grease and flour 9 x 5 x 3-inch loaf pan. Cut butter and cream cheese into 1-inch slices; place in bowl of food processor. Add sugar; process until smooth, about 30 seconds. Add eggs, vanilla and orange peel; process until blended, about 10 seconds. Add flour and baking powder; process until blended, about 10 seconds. Stir in MINI CHIPS Chocolate. Pour batter into prepared pan. Bake 45 to 50 minutes or until cake pulls away from sides of pan. Cool 10 minutes; remove from pan to wire racks. Cool completely; sprinkle confectioners' sugar over cake.

About 10 servings

Ice Cream Sundae Cake Ⓣ

- 1 package (18.25 to 18.75 ounces) cake mix, any flavor
- 1 can (16 ounces) HERSHEY'S Chocolate Fudge Topping, at room temperature
  Ice Cream

Prepare and bake cake according to package directions for 13 x 9 x 2-inch baking pan. Remove from oven; immediately place heaping tablespoonfuls of fudge topping on cake. Let stand 15 minutes or until fudge topping is soft enough to spread. Gently spread evenly over cake. Serve slightly warm or cool, with scoops of ice cream.   *12 to 15 servings*

Chocolate Chip Orange Pound Cake

13

Chocolate Stripe Cake 🍫 🌙

1 package (18.25 ounces)
   white cake mix
1 envelope unflavored gelatin
1/4 cup cold water
1/4 cup boiling water
1 cup HERSHEY'S Syrup
   Whipped topping
   HERSHEY'S Syrup (optional
   garnish)

Heat oven to 350°. Grease and flour 13 × 9 × 2-inch baking pan. Prepare cake batter and bake according to package directions. Cool 15 minutes. Do not remove cake from pan. With fork, carefully pierce cake to bottom of pan, making rows about 1 inch apart covering length and width of cake. In small bowl sprinkle gelatin over cold water; let stand 1 minute to soften. Add boiling water; stir until gelatin is completely dissolved and mixture is clear. Stir in 1 cup syrup. Pour chocolate mixture evenly over cooled cake, making sure entire top is covered and mixture has flowed into holes. Cover; chill about 5 hours or until set. Serve with whipped topping; garnish with syrup, if desired. Refrigerate leftovers. *12 to 15 servings*

Cream-Filled Banana Cupcakes 🍫

Cream Cheese Filling
   (recipe follows)
1 package (18.5 ounces)
   banana cake mix (with
   pudding in the mix)
3/4 cup finely chopped nuts
2 tablespoons sugar

Prepare Cream Cheese Filling; set aside. Heat oven to 350°. Prepare cake batter according to package directions. Fill paper-lined muffin cups (2 1/2 inches in diameter) 1/2 full with batter. Spoon about 1 teaspoonful filling into center of each cupcake. Combine nuts and sugar; sprinkle about 1 teaspoonful over top of each cupcake. Bake 20 minutes or until wooden pick inserted in cake portion comes out clean. Cool on wire rack.
About 3 dozen cupcakes

Cream Cheese Filling

1 package (8 ounces) cream
   cheese, softened
1/3 cup sugar
1 egg
1 cup HERSHEY'S MINI CHIPS
   Semi-Sweet Chocolate

In small mixer bowl combine cream cheese, sugar and egg; beat until smooth. Stir in MINI CHIPS Chocolate.

Chocolate Stripe Cake (top) and Cream-Filled Banana Cupcakes (bottom)

Banana Chip Bundt Cake ⬡

- 1 package (18.5 ounces) banana cake mix (with pudding in the mix)
- 1 package (3½ ounces) instant banana cream pudding and pie filling
- 4 eggs
- 1 cup water
- ½ cup vegetable oil
- 1 cup HERSHEY'S MINI CHIPS Semi-Sweet Chocolate Chocolate Glaze (recipe follows)

Heat oven to 350°. Grease and flour 12-cup Bundt pan. In large mixer bowl combine cake mix, pudding mix, eggs, water and oil; beat on low speed just until blended. Increase speed to medium; beat 2 minutes. Stir in MINI CHIPS Chocolate. Pour batter into prepared pan. Bake 45 to 50 minutes or until wooden pick inserted in center comes out clean. Cool 10 minutes; remove from pan. Cool completely on wire rack. Drizzle with Chocolate Glaze.   *12 to 16 servings*

Chocolate Glaze ⬤

In small saucepan bring ⅓ cup sugar and ¼ cup water to full boil, stirring until sugar dissolves. Remove from heat; add 1 cup HERSHEY'S MINI CHIPS Semi-Sweet Chocolate. Stir with wire whisk until chips are melted and mixture is smooth. Cool to desired consistency; use immediately.

About ⅔ cup glaze

Chocolatetown Special Cake ◑

1/2 cup HERSHEY'S Cocoa
1/2 cup boiling water
2/3 cup shortening
1 3/4 cups sugar
1 teaspoon vanilla extract
2 eggs
2 1/4 cups all-purpose flour
1 1/2 teaspoons baking soda
1/2 teaspoon salt
1 1/3 cups buttermilk or sour milk*
One-Bowl Buttercream Frosting (recipe page 90)

In small bowl stir together cocoa and boiling water until smooth; set aside. Heat oven to 350°. Grease and flour two 9-inch round baking pans. In large mixer bowl cream shortening, sugar and vanilla until light and fluffy. Add eggs; beat well. Combine flour, baking soda and salt; add alternately with buttermilk to creamed mixture. Blend in cocoa mixture. Pour into prepared pans. Bake 35 to 40 minutes or until wooden pick inserted in center comes out clean. Cool 10 minutes; remove from pans. Cool completely; frost with One-Bowl Buttercream Frosting. Garnish as desired.
10 to 12 servings

*To sour milk: Use 1 tablespoon plus 1 teaspoon white vinegar plus milk to equal 1 1/3 cups.

Chocolate Sour Cream Cake

1 3/4 cups all-purpose flour
1 3/4 cups sugar
3/4 cup HERSHEY'S Cocoa
1 1/2 teaspoons baking soda
1 teaspoon salt
2/3 cup butter or margarine, softened
2 cups dairy sour cream
2 eggs
1 teaspoon vanilla extract
Fudge Frosting (recipe follows)

Heat oven to 350°. Grease and flour 13 x 9 x 2-inch baking pan. In large mixer bowl combine flour, sugar, cocoa, baking soda and salt. Blend in butter, sour cream, eggs and vanilla. Beat 3 minutes on medium speed. Pour batter into prepared pan. Bake 40 to 45 minutes or until wooden pick inserted in center comes out clean. Cool in pan on wire rack. Frost with Fudge Frosting.
12 to 15 servings

Fudge Frosting

3 tablespoons butter or margarine
1/3 cup HERSHEY'S Cocoa
1 1/3 cups confectioners' sugar
2 to 3 tablespoons milk
1/2 teaspoon vanilla extract

In small saucepan over low heat melt butter. Add cocoa; cook, stirring constantly, just until mixture begins to boil. Pour mixture into small mixer bowl; cool completely. To cocoa mixture, add confectioners' sugar alternately with milk, beating to spreading consistency. Blend in vanilla.
About 1 cup frosting

Cool DESSERTS

Soothing, refreshing desserts for everyday or for entertaining guests.

From left to right: Chocolate Mint Dessert (recipe page 23),Creamy Smooth Choco-Blueberry Parfaits (recipe page 20) and Easy Double Chocolate Ice Cream (recipe page 25)

Chocolate-Covered Banana Pops ◖

3 ripe, large bananas
9 wooden ice cream sticks or skewers
2 cups (12-ounce package) HERSHEY'S Semi-Sweet Chocolate Chips
2 tablespoons shortening
1½ cups coarsely chopped unsalted, roasted peanuts

Peel bananas; cut each into thirds. Insert wooden stick into each banana piece; place on wax paper-covered tray. Cover; freeze until firm. In top of double boiler over hot, not boiling, water melt chocolate chips and shortening. Remove bananas from freezer just before dipping. Dip each piece into warm chocolate, covering completely; allow excess to drip off. Immediately roll in peanuts. Cover; return to freezer. Serve frozen.   *9 pops*

Creamy Smooth Choco-Blueberry Parfaits ▢

1 package (6 ounces) instant chocolate pudding and pie filling
2 cups milk
½ cup HERSHEY'S Syrup
3½ cups (8-ounce container) frozen non-dairy whipped topping, thawed
1¾ cups canned blueberry pie filling, chilled

Chocolate-Covered Banana Pops

In large mixer bowl combine pudding mix, milk and syrup; mix well. In separate bowl fold whipped topping into blueberry pie filling; reserve about 1 cup for garnish. Beginning with chocolate mixture, alternately layer with blueberry topping in parfait glasses. Cover and chill. Top with reserved blueberry topping. Garnish as desired.

6 to 8 parfaits

Banana Fudge Pops

1 ripe, medium banana
1¹/₂ cups orange-banana juice
¹/₂ cup sugar
¹/₄ cup HERSHEY'S Cocoa
1 can (5 ounces) evaporated milk
6 paper cold drink cups (5 ounces each)
6 wooden popsicle sticks

Slice banana into blender container; add juice. Cover; blend until smooth. Add sugar and cocoa; cover and blend well. Add evaporated milk; cover and blend. Pour mixture into cups. Freeze about 1 hour; insert popsicle sticks into fudge pops. Cover; freeze until firm. Peel off cups to serve.

6 pops

Banana Fudge Pops

Choco-Berry Frozen Dessert

Choco-Berry Frozen Dessert

- **3 packages (3 ounces each) cream cheese, softened and divided**
- **1 cup HERSHEY'S Syrup**
- **1/2 cup water**
- **4 1/2 cups (about 12 ounces) frozen non-dairy whipped topping, thawed and divided**
- **3/4 cup pureed strawberries (fresh, sweetened OR frozen, thawed and drained berries)**

Line 9×5×3-inch loaf pan with foil. In large mixer bowl beat 2 packages cream cheese. Blend in syrup and water; beat until smooth. Fold in 3 cups whipped topping. Spoon half of chocolate mixture into prepared pan; freeze 15 minutes. Chill remaining chocolate mixture. In small mixer bowl beat remaining package cream cheese. Blend in strawberries until smooth. Fold in remaining 1 1/2 cups whipped topping. Spoon strawberry mixture over chocolate layer in pan. Top with chilled chocolate mixture. Cover; freeze several hours or overnight until firm. Unmold about 10 minutes before serving. Peel off foil before slicing.

About 10 servings

Cherry-Crowned Cocoa Pudding

- **1 cup sugar**
- **1/2 cup HERSHEY'S Cocoa**
- **1/3 cup all-purpose biscuit baking mix**
- **2 cups milk**
- **1 cup water**
- **1 can (21 ounces) cherry pie filling, chilled**

In medium saucepan combine sugar, cocoa and baking mix. Stir in milk and water. Cook over medium heat, stirring constantly, until mixture comes to full boil; remove from heat. Pour into dessert dishes. Press plastic wrap directly onto surface. Chill several hours or until set. Garnish with cherry pie filling. *6 servings*

Cherry-Crowned Cocoa Pudding

Chocolate Mint Dessert ◖

1 cup all-purpose flour
1 cup sugar
1/2 cup butter or margarine, softened
4 eggs
1 1/2 cups (16-ounce can) HERSHEY'S Syrup
Mint Cream Center (recipe follows)
Chocolate Topping (recipe follows)

Heat oven to 350°. Grease 13 x 9 x 2-inch baking pan. In large mixer bowl combine flour, sugar, butter, eggs and syrup; beat until smooth. Pour into prepared pan; bake 25 to 30 minutes or until top springs back when touched lightly. Cool completely in pan. Spread Mint Cream Center on cake; cover and chill. Pour Chocolate Topping over chilled dessert. Cover; chill at least 1 hour before serving.
About 12 servings

Mint Cream Center

2 cups confectioners' sugar
1/2 cup butter or margarine, softened
2 tablespoons green creme de menthe*

In small mixer bowl combine confectioners' sugar, butter and creme de menthe; beat until smooth.

*1 tablespoon water, 1/2 to 3/4 teaspoon mint extract and 3 drops green food color may be substituted for creme de menthe.

Chocolate Topping

6 tablespoons butter or margarine
1 cup HERSHEY'S Semi-Sweet Chocolate Chips

In small saucepan over very low heat melt butter and chocolate chips. Remove from heat; stir until smooth. Cool slightly.

Easy Chocolate Sprinkled Ice Cream

3 egg yolks
1 can (14 ounces) sweetened condensed milk
3 tablespoons water
1 tablespoon vanilla extract
1 cup HERSHEY'S MINI CHIPS Semi-Sweet Chocolate
2 cups chilled whipping cream

Line 9 x 5 x 3-inch loaf pan with foil. In large bowl beat egg yolks with wire whisk; stir in sweetened condensed milk, water and vanilla. Finely chop MINI CHIPS Chocolate by hand or in food processor; set aside. In large mixer bowl beat whipping cream until stiff; fold with chopped chocolate into egg yolk mixture. Pour into prepared pan. Cover; freeze 6 hours or until firm.

About 6 servings

Skor Toffee Candy Bar Ice Cream

3 egg yolks
1 can (14 ounces) sweetened condensed milk
3 tablespoons water
1 tablespoon vanilla extract
5 bars (1.4 ounces each) SKOR Toffee Candy Bar
2 cups chilled whipping cream

Line 9 x 5 x 3-inch loaf pan with foil. In large bowl beat egg yolks with wire whisk; stir in sweetened condensed milk, water and vanilla. Finely chop SKOR bars by hand or in food processor to measure 1¼ cups; set aside. In large mixer bowl beat whipping cream until stiff; fold with chopped SKOR Bars into egg yolk mixture. Pour into prepared pan. Cover; freeze 6 hours or until firm.

6 servings

24

Chocolate Rum Ice Cream

- 1 cup sugar
- 2 tablespoons all-purpose flour
- 1 cup milk
- 1 egg, slightly beaten
- 2 squares (2 ounces) HERSHEY'S Unsweetened Baking Chocolate, broken into pieces
- 1/2 teaspoon rum extract
- 2 cups chilled light cream

In large microwave-safe bowl combine sugar and flour; gradually stir in milk. Blend in egg and baking chocolate pieces. Microwave at HIGH (100%) 2 to 2 1/2 minutes, stirring frequently, just until mixture boils and thickens. Add rum extract; blend with whisk until mixture is smooth. Chill thoroughly. Add light cream to chilled mixture; blend well. Freeze in 2-quart ice cream freezer according to manufacturer's directions.   *About 8 servings*

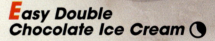

Chocolate Rum Ice Cream

Easy Double Chocolate Ice Cream

- 2 cups chilled whipping cream
- 2 tablespoons HERSHEY'S Cocoa
- 1 can (14 ounces) sweetened condensed milk
- 1/3 cup HERSHEY'S Syrup

Line 9 x 5 x 3-inch loaf pan with foil. In large mixer bowl beat whipping cream and cocoa until stiff. Combine sweetened condensed milk and syrup; fold into whipped cream mixture. Pour into prepared pan. Cover; freeze 6 hours or until firm.

About 6 servings

No-Bake Chocolate Cake Roll 🍵 🌙 ⚅

1 package (3½ ounces) instant vanilla pudding and pie filling
3 tablespoons HERSHEY'S Cocoa, divided
1 cup milk
3½ cups (8-ounce container) frozen non-dairy whipped topping, thawed and divided
1 package (8½ ounces) chocolate wafers (about 42)

In small mixer bowl combine pudding mix and 2 tablespoons cocoa. Add milk; beat on low speed until smooth and thickened. Fold in 1 cup whipped topping; blend well. Spread about 1 tablespoon pudding mixture onto each chocolate wafer. On foil, stack wafers on edges to form one long roll. Wrap tightly; chill at least 5 hours or overnight. Sift remaining 1 tablespoon cocoa over remaining 2½ cups whipped topping; blend well. Cover; chill until just before serving. Unwrap roll; place on serving tray. Spread reserved whipped topping mixture over entire roll. To serve, cut diagonally in slices. Store, covered, in refrigerator. Garnish as desired. *About 8 servings*

Fudgey Decadence Pudding 🌙 🌊

2 squares (2 ounces) HERSHEY'S Unsweetened Baking Chocolate, finely chopped
1 cup light cream
²/₃ cup sugar
2 egg yolks, slightly beaten
2 tablespoons butter or margarine
1 teaspoon vanilla extract

In medium microwave-safe bowl combine baking chocolate pieces and light cream. Microwave at HIGH (100%) 1½ to 2 minutes or just until mixture is smooth when stirred. Microwave at HIGH about 1 minute or until mixture just begins to boil; stir in sugar. Microwave at HIGH about 1 minute or just until mixture begins to boil. With wire whisk gradually stir in beaten egg yolks; stir in butter and vanilla, blending well. Pour into creme pots or demitasse cups; press plastic wrap directly onto surface. Chill several hours or until set. Garnish as desired.
6 servings

No-Bake Chocolate Cake Roll

Chocolate-Marshmallow Mousse 🌓 Ⓝ

1 bar (8 ounces) HERSHEY'S
    Milk Chocolate Bar
1½ cups miniature
    marshmallows
⅓ cup milk
1 cup chilled whipping cream

Break chocolate bar into pieces;
place in medium microwave-safe
bowl with marshmallows and milk.
Microwave at HIGH (100%) 1 to 1½
minutes or just until mixture is
smooth when stirred; cool to room
temperature. In small mixer bowl
beat whipping cream until stiff;
fold into cooled chocolate
mixture. Pour into dessert dishes.
Cover; chill 1 to 2 hours or until
set. *6 servings*

VARIATIONS
**Chocolate-Marshmallow
Mousse Parfaits:** Prepare
Chocolate-Marshmallow Mousse
according to directions.
Alternately spoon mousse and
sweetened whipped cream or
whipped topping into parfait
glasses. Cover; chill about 1 hour.
4 to 6 servings

Chocolate-Marshmallow 🅜
Mousse Pie: Prepare Microwave
Chocolate Crumb Crust (recipe
follows) or use 8-inch (6 ounces)
packaged chocolate flavored
crumb crust. Prepare Chocolate-
Marshmallow Mousse according
to directions. Pour into crust. Cover;
chill 2 to 3 hours or until firm.
Garnish as desired. *8 servings*

Microwave Chocolate Ⓝ Crumb Crust

Grease microwave-safe 9-inch pie
plate. In small microwave-safe
bowl place ½ cup butter or
margarine. Microwave at HIGH
(100%) about 1 minute or until
melted. Stir in 1½ cups graham
cracker crumbs, 6 tablespoons
HERSHEY'S Cocoa and ⅓ cup
confectioners' sugar until well
blended. Press onto bottom and
up sides of prepared pie plate.
Microwave at HIGH 1 to 1½
minutes or until blistered; *do not
overcook.* Cool completely before
filling.

Fast Fudge Pots de Creme 🌓

1 package (3½ ounces)
    chocolate pudding and
    pie filling
2 cups milk
1 cup HERSHEY'S Semi-Sweet
    Chocolate Chips or MINI
    CHIPS

In medium saucepan combine
pudding mix and milk. Cook over
medium heat, stirring constantly,
until mixture comes to full boil;
remove from heat. Stir in
chocolate chips until melted and
mixture is smooth. Spoon into 8
creme pots or demitasse cups.
Press plastic wrap directly onto
surface. Serve slightly warm or
chilled. Garnish as desired.
8 servings

Chocolate Frozen Dessert ◐

1 package (16 ounces) chocolate sandwich cookies, crushed (about 1³/₄ cups)
¹/₂ cup butter or margarine, melted
¹/₂ gallon vanilla ice cream (in rectangular block)
Chocolate Sauce (recipe follows)
²/₃ cup pecan pieces (optional)

In medium bowl combine crushed cookies and butter. Press mixture onto bottom of 13 × 9 × 2-inch pan or two 8-inch square pans. Cut ice cream into ¹/₂-inch slices; place over crust. Cover; freeze 1 to 2 hours or until firm.

Uncover pan(s); pour Chocolate Sauce over ice cream. Sprinkle pecan pieces over top, if desired. Cover; freeze until firm.
About 16 to 18 servings

Chocolate Sauce

2 cups confectioners' sugar
¹/₂ cup butter or margarine
1¹/₂ cups (12-ounce can) evaporated milk
1 cup HERSHEY'S Semi-Sweet Chocolate Chips

In medium saucepan combine confectioners' sugar, butter, evaporated milk and chocolate chips. Cook over medium heat, stirring constantly, until mixture boils; boil and stir 8 minutes. Remove from heat; cool slightly.
About 2¹/₂ cups

Pies

A tantalizing
selection of pies—
all easy to make,
and easy to enjoy.

Chocolate Grasshopper Pie
(recipe page 32)

Chocolate Grasshopper Pie 🌓 ❷

Microwave Chocolate
  Crumb Crust (recipe
  follows) OR
  8-inch (6 ounces)
  packaged chocolate
  flavored crumb crust
3 cups miniature
  marshmallows
1/2 cup milk
1/4 cup HERSHEY'S Cocoa
2 tablespoons white creme
  de menthe
2 tablespoons white creme
  de cacao
1 cup chilled whipping cream
2 tablespoons confectioners'
  sugar

Prepare crust, if desired; set aside.
In medium saucepan combine
marshmallows, milk and cocoa.
Stir constantly over low heat until
marshmallows are melted; remove
from heat. Stir in creme de
menthe and creme de cacao;
cool to room temperature. In large
mixer bowl beat whipping cream
with confectioners' sugar until stiff.
Fold in cooled chocolate mixture.
Spoon into crust. Cover and freeze
several hours or overnight. Garnish
as desired.   *6 to 8 servings*

Microwave Chocolate Ⓝ Crumb Crust

Grease microwave-safe 9-inch pie
plate. In small microwave-safe
bowl place 1/2 cup butter or
margarine. Microwave at HIGH
(100%) about 1 minute or until
melted. Stir in 1 1/2 cups graham
cracker crumbs, 6 tablespoons
HERSHEY'S Cocoa and 1/3 cup
confectioners' sugar until well
blended. Press onto bottom and
up sides of prepared pie plate.
Microwave at HIGH 1 to 1 1/2
minutes or until blistered; *do not
overcook.* Cool completely before
filling.

Chocolate Mousse Pie 🌓 ❷

1 envelope unflavored gelatin
2 tablespoons cold water
1/4 cup boiling water
1 cup sugar
1/2 cup HERSHEY'S Cocoa
2 cups chilled whipping
  cream
2 teaspoons vanilla extract
  8-inch (6 ounces) packaged
  chocolate flavored crumb
  crust

In small bowl sprinkle gelatin over
cold water; let stand 5 minutes to
soften. Add boiling water; stir until
gelatin is completely dissolved
and mixture is clear. Cool slightly.
In large mixer bowl stir together
sugar and cocoa; add whipping
cream and vanilla. Beat on
medium speed, scraping bottom
of bowl often, until stiff. Pour
gelatin mixture into whipped
cream; beat until well blended.
Spoon into crust. Cover; chill at
least 2 hours. Garnish as desired.
          6 to 8 servings

Hershey's Syrup Pie ◐ ◎

9-inch baked pastry shell
2 egg yolks
¹/₃ cup cornstarch
¹/₄ teaspoon salt
1³/₄ cups milk
1 cup HERSHEY'S Syrup
1 teaspoon vanilla extract
Syrup Whipped Topping
(recipe follows)
Fresh fruit

Prepare pastry shell; cool. In medium microwave-safe bowl beat egg yolks. Add cornstarch, salt, milk and syrup; blend well. Microwave at MEDIUM-HIGH (70%) 6 to 8 minutes, stirring every 2 minutes with whisk, or until mixture is smooth and very thick. Stir in vanilla. Pour into baked pastry shell. Press plastic wrap directly onto surface; chill several hours or overnight. Garnish with Syrup Whipped Topping and fresh fruit.

6 to 8 servings

Syrup Whipped Topping ✪

In small mixer bowl combine 1 cup chilled whipping cream, ¹/₂ cup HERSHEY'S Syrup, 2 tablespoons confectioners' sugar and ¹/₂ teaspoon vanilla extract. Beat just until cream holds definite shape; *do not overbeat.*

About 2¹/₄ cups topping

Two-Tone Cream Pie ◐ ⬭

9-inch baked pastry shell
1 package (4³/₄ ounces) vanilla pudding and pie filling
3¹/₂ cups milk
1 cup REESE'S Peanut Butter Chips
1 cup HERSHEY'S Semi-Sweet Chocolate Chips or MINI CHIPS

Prepare pastry shell; cool. In medium saucepan combine pudding mix and milk. Cook over medium heat, stirring constantly, until mixture comes to full boil; remove from heat. Pour 2 cups hot pudding into small bowl and add peanut butter chips; stir until chips are melted and mixture is smooth. To remaining hot pudding, add chocolate chips; stir until chips are melted and mixture is smooth. Pour chocolate mixture into baked pastry shell. Gently pour and spread peanut butter mixture over top. Press plastic wrap directly onto surface. Chill several hours or overnight. Garnish as desired.

8 servings

Chocolate Chip Walnut Pie

9-inch baked pastry shell
³/₄ cup packed light brown sugar
¹/₂ cup all-purpose flour
¹/₂ teaspoon baking powder
¹/₄ teaspoon ground cinnamon
2 eggs, slightly beaten
1 cup HERSHEY'S Semi-Sweet Chocolate Chips, MINI CHIPS or Milk Chocolate Chips
1 cup coarsely chopped walnuts
Spiced Cream (recipe page 93)

Prepare pastry shell; cool. Heat oven to 350°. In medium bowl combine brown sugar, flour, baking powder and cinnamon. Add eggs; stir until well blended. Add chocolate chips and walnuts. Pour into baked pastry shell. Bake 25 to 30 minutes or until lightly browned and set. Serve slightly warm or at room temperature with Spiced Cream.

8 servings

Chocolate Chip Walnut Pie

Double Chocolate Mocha Pie

Peanut Butter Cream Pie

1 package (3½ ounces) instant vanilla pudding and pie filling
1 cup dairy sour cream
1 cup milk
1½ cups REESE'S Peanut Butter Chips
2 tablespoons vegetable oil
8-Inch (6 ounces) packaged crumb crust
Whipped topping

In small mixer bowl blend pudding mix, sour cream and milk; set aside. In top of double boiler over hot, not boiling, water melt peanut butter chips with oil, stirring constantly to blend. OR in small microwave-safe bowl place chips and oil. Microwave at HIGH (100%) 45 seconds; stir. If necessary, microwave at HIGH additional 15 seconds or until melted and smooth when stirred. Gradually add to pudding, blending well. Pour into crust. Cover; chill several hours or overnight. Garnish with whipped topping.   *6 to 8 servings*

Double Chocolate Mocha Pie

1 package (6 ounces) instant chocolate pudding and pie filling
2⅔ cups HERSHEY'S Chocolate Milk
8-inch (6 ounces) packaged crumb crust
Coffee Whipped Cream (recipe follows)

In large mixer bowl beat pudding mix and chocolate milk until blended. Pour into crust. Cover and chill several hours or overnight. Serve with dollops of Coffee Whipped Cream. Garnish as desired.   *6 to 8 servings*

Coffee Whipped Cream
In small mixer bowl combine 1 cup chilled whipping cream, ¼ cup confectioners' sugar, 1 tablespoon powdered instant coffee and ½ teaspoon vanilla extract. Beat just until cream holds definite shape; *do not overbeat.*
           About 2 cups topping

Cocoa Cloud Pie

2 packages (3 ounces each)
    cream cheese, softened
1 cup confectioners' sugar
2 teaspoons vanilla extract
1/2 cup HERSHEY'S Cocoa
1/4 cup milk
2 cups chilled whipping
    cream
    8-inch (6 ounces) packaged
    crumb crust

In large mixer bowl beat cream
cheese, confectioners' sugar and
vanilla until well blended. Add
cocoa alternately with milk,
beating until smooth. Gradually
add whipping cream, beating
until stiff. Spoon into crust. Cover;
chill several hours or overnight.
Garnish as desired.

6 to 8 servings

Peanut Butter Tarts

1 package (3 1/2 ounces)
    instant vanilla pudding
    and pie filling
1 1/2 cups milk, divided
1 cup REESE'S Peanut Butter
    Chips
6 (4-ounce package) single
    serve graham crusts
    Whipped topping
    Fresh fruit

In small mixer bowl blend
pudding mix and 1 cup milk; set
aside. In top of double boiler over
hot, not boiling, water melt peanut

*From top to bottom: Cocoa Cloud
Pie, Peanut Butter Tarts and Individual
Chocolate Cream Pies*

butter chips with remaining 1/2
cup milk, stirring constantly to
blend. OR in small microwave-safe
bowl place chips and 1/2 cup
milk. Microwave at HIGH (100%) 45
seconds; stir. If necessary,
microwave at HIGH additional 15
seconds or until melted and
smooth when stirred. Gradually
add to pudding, blending well.
Spoon into crusts. Cover; chill until
set. Garnish with whipped topping
and fruit.   *6 servings*

Individual Chocolate Cream Pies

1 1/2 ounces (1/2 of 3-ounce
    package) cream cheese,
    softened
6 tablespoons sugar
1/2 teaspoon vanilla extract
2 1/2 tablespoons HERSHEY'S
    Cocoa
2 1/2 tablespoons milk
1 cup chilled whipping cream
6 (4-ounce package) single
    serve graham crusts
    Whipped topping
    HERSHEY'S MINI CHIPS Semi-
    Sweet Chocolate

In small mixer bowl beat cream
cheese, sugar and vanilla until
well blended. Add cocoa
alternately with milk, beating until
smooth. In separate bowl beat
whipping cream until stiff; fold into
chocolate mixture. Spoon into
crusts. Cover; chill until set.
Garnish with whipped topping
and MINI CHIPS Chocolate.

6 servings

Fudge Satin Pie

1 cup HERSHEY'S Semi-Sweet Chocolate Chips or MINI CHIPS
4 eggs, separated and at room temperature
1/4 teaspoon cream of tartar
1/4 cup sugar
1 teaspoon vanilla extract
   8-inch (6 ounces) packaged crumb crust
   Whipped topping
   Chocolate curls

In top of double boiler over hot, not boiling, water melt chocolate chips, stirring constantly to blend. OR in small microwave-safe bowl place chips. Microwave at HIGH (100%) 1 minute; stir. If necessary, microwave at HIGH additional 15 seconds or until melted and smooth when stirred. In small mixer bowl slightly beat egg yolks. Gradually add melted chocolate, beating well after each addition; set aside. Using clean beaters and large mixer bowl, beat egg whites and cream of tartar until foamy. Gradually add sugar and vanilla, beating until stiff peaks form. Fold in chocolate mixture. Pour into crust. Cover; chill several hours or overnight. Garnish with whipped topping and chocolate curls.
6 to 8 servings

Double Chocolate Pie

1 package (6 ounces) instant chocolate pudding and pie filling
2²/3 cups HERSHEY'S Chocolate Milk
   8-inch (6 ounces) packaged crumb crust
   Whipped topping

In large mixer bowl beat pudding mix and chocolate milk until blended. Pour into crust. Cover; chill several hours or overnight. Garnish with whipped topping.
6 to 8 servings

Smooth-n-Rich Chocolate Pie

1 cup confectioners' sugar
1/2 cup butter, softened
5 squares (5 ounces) HERSHEY'S Semi-Sweet Baking Chocolate, melted and cooled
1 teaspoon vanilla extract
2 eggs
1/2 cup chilled whipping cream
   8-inch (6 ounces) packaged graham cracker crumb crust

In small mixer bowl combine confectioners' sugar and butter; beat until light and fluffy. Blend in cooled chocolate and vanilla; beat in eggs. In separate bowl beat whipping cream until stiff; fold into chocolate mixture. Spoon into crust. Cover; freeze until firm.
6 to 8 servings

Chocolate Cheese Pie

Chocolate Cheese Pie

- 1 package (8 ounces) cream cheese, softened
- 1 package (3 ounces) cream cheese, softened
- 3/4 cup sugar
- 1 teaspoon vanilla extract
- 1/4 cup HERSHEY'S Cocoa
- 2 eggs
- 1/2 cup whipping cream
- 8-inch (6 ounces) packaged crumb crust
- Cherry pie or peach pie filling

Heat oven to 350°. In large mixer bowl beat cream cheese, sugar and vanilla until well blended. Blend in cocoa, scraping sides of bowl and beaters frequently. Add eggs; blend well. Blend in whipping cream. Pour into crust. Bake 35 to 40 minutes. (Center will be soft but will set upon cooling.) Cool to room temperature. Cover; chill several hours or overnight. Serve with pie filling.

6 to 8 servings

Chocolate Pecan Pie

- 9-inch unbaked pastry shell
- 1 cup sugar
- 1/3 cup HERSHEY'S Cocoa
- 3 eggs, slightly beaten
- 1 cup light corn syrup
- 1 tablespoon butter or margarine, melted
- 1 teaspoon vanilla extract
- 1 cup pecan halves
- Whipped topping

Prepare pastry shell; set aside. Heat oven to 350°. In medium bowl combine sugar and cocoa. Add eggs, corn syrup, butter and vanilla; stir until well blended. Stir in pecans. Pour into unbaked pastry shell. Bake 60 minutes. Cool completely. Garnish with whipped topping.

8 servings

BREADS, MUFFINS COFFEECAKES

Let the irresistible aroma of these breads and coffeecakes fill your kitchen.

From top to bottom: Chocolate Chip Banana Bread (recipe page 42) and Quick Cocoa-Bran Muffins (recipe page 43)

Chocolate Streusel & Spice Coffeecake Ⓣ

1 package (10 to 13 ounces) fruit, cinnamon, spice or bran muffin mix
1/2 cup HERSHEY'S Semi-Sweet Chocolate Chips
3/4 cup confectioners' sugar
1/2 cup chopped nuts
1/4 cup HERSHEY'S Cocoa
3 tablespoons butter or margarine, melted

Heat oven to 350°. Grease bottom only of 9-inch square baking pan. Prepare muffin mix as directed; stir in chocolate chips. Pour into prepared pan. In small bowl combine confectioners' sugar, nuts and cocoa; with fork stir in butter until crumbly. Sprinkle over batter. Bake 25 to 30 minutes or until wooden pick inserted in center comes out clean. Cool.

9 servings

Chocolate Chip Banana Bread

2 cups all-purpose flour
1 cup sugar
1 teaspoon baking powder
1/2 teaspoon baking soda
1 teaspoon salt
1 cup mashed ripe bananas (about 3 small)
1/2 cup shortening
2 eggs
1 cup HERSHEY'S Semi-Sweet Chocolate Chips
1/2 cup chopped walnuts

Heat oven to 350°. Grease bottoms only of two 8 1/2 x 4 1/2 x 2 1/2-inch loaf pans. In large mixer bowl combine all ingredients except chocolate chips and walnuts; blend well on medium speed. Stir in chips and walnuts. Pour into prepared pans. Bake 45 to 50 minutes or until wooden pick inserted in center comes out clean. Cool 10 minutes; remove from pans to wire rack. Cool completely.

2 loaves

Chocolate Streusel & Spice Coffeecake

Quick Cocoa-Bran Muffins

- 1 package (10.75 ounces) bran and honey muffin mix
- 1/4 cup HERSHEY'S Cocoa
- 1 egg, slightly beaten
- 3/4 cup water
- 1/2 cup raisins
- 1/2 cup finely chopped nuts (optional)

Heat oven to 400°. Grease or paper-line 12 muffin cups (2½ inches in diameter). In large bowl combine muffin mix and cocoa. Stir in egg and water just until blended. Stir in raisins and nuts, if desired. Fill muffin cups 3/4 full with batter. Bake 15 to 17 minutes or until wooden pick inserted in center comes out clean. Serve warm.   *About 1 dozen muffins*

Easy Chocolate Zucchini Cake

- 1 package (16.1 ounces) nut quick bread mix
- 1/2 cup sugar
- 1 teaspoon ground cinnamon
- 3/4 cup vegetable oil
- 3 eggs, slightly beaten
- 1½ cups shredded zucchini
- 1 cup HERSHEY'S Semi-Sweet Chocolate Chips
  Confectioners' sugar (optional)

Heat oven to 350°. Grease and flour 9-inch square baking pan. In large bowl combine bread mix, sugar, cinnamon, oil and eggs; mix until well blended. Stir in zucchini and chocolate chips; pour into prepared pan. Bake 40 to 45 minutes or until wooden pick inserted in center comes out clean. Cool. Sprinkle confectioners' sugar over top, if desired. Cover; refrigerate leftovers.   *9 servings*

Easy Chocolate Zucchini Cake

43

*C*hocolate Chip Fruit Muffins 🖘

- 1 package (15 ounces) banana quick bread mix
- 2 eggs, slightly beaten
- 1 cup milk
- 1/4 cup vegetable oil
- 1 cup HERSHEY'S Semi-Sweet Chocolate Chips, MINI CHIPS or Milk Chocolate Chips
- 1/2 cup dried fruit bits

Heat oven to 400°. Grease or paper-line 18 muffin cups (2 1/2 inches in diameter). In large bowl combine bread mix, eggs, milk and oil. Beat with spoon 30 seconds. Stir in chocolate chips and fruit bits. Fill muffin cups 3/4 full with batter. Bake 18 to 20 minutes or until lightly browned. Serve warm.

About 1 1/2 dozen muffins

*M*ini Chips Surprise Muffins 🖘

- 1 package (16.1 ounces) nut quick bread mix
- 1 egg, slightly beaten
- 1 cup milk
- 1/4 cup vegetable oil
- 1 cup HERSHEY'S MINI CHIPS Semi-Sweet Chocolate
- 1/3 cup fruit preserves, any flavor

Chocolate Chip Fruit Muffins (top) and Mini Chips Surprise Muffins (bottom)

Heat oven to 400°. Grease or paper-line 18 muffin cups (2½ inches in diameter). In large bowl combine bread mix, egg, milk and oil. Beat with spoon 1 minute. Stir in MINI CHIPS Chocolate. Fill muffin cups ¼ full with batter. Spoon ½ teaspoon preserves onto center of batter. Fill muffin cups ¾ full with batter. Bake 20 to 22 minutes or until lightly browned. Serve warm.

About 1½ dozen muffins

Mini Chips Cinnamon Crescents

1 can (8 ounces) refrigerated
    quick crescent dinner rolls
Ground cinnamon
½ cup HERSHEY'S MINI CHIPS
    Semi-Sweet Chocolate
    Confectioners' sugar

Heat oven to 375°. On ungreased cookie sheet unroll dough to form 8 triangles. Lightly sprinkle cinnamon and 1 tablespoon MINI CHIPS Chocolate on top of each. Gently press into dough to adhere. Starting at shortest side of triangle, roll dough to opposite point. Bake 10 to 12 minutes or until golden brown. Sprinkle confectioners' sugar over top. Serve warm.

8 crescents

Mini Chips Cinnamon Crescents

Chocolate Sticky Bubble Loaf

- 2 loaves frozen bread dough, thawed
- 3/4 cup granulated sugar
- 4 tablespoons HERSHEY'S Cocoa, divided
- 1 teaspoon ground cinnamon
- 1/2 cup butter or margarine, melted and divided
- 1/4 cup water
- 1/2 cup packed light brown sugar
- 1/2 cup pecan pieces

Thaw loaves as directed on package; let rise until doubled. In small bowl combine granulated sugar, 1 tablespoon cocoa and cinnamon; set aside. In small microwave-safe bowl combine 1/4 cup melted butter, water, brown sugar and remaining 3 tablespoons cocoa; microwave at HIGH (100%) 30 to 60 seconds or until smooth when stirred. Pour mixture into 12-cup Bundt pan; sprinkle with pecan pieces. Heat oven to 350°. Pinch off pieces of bread dough; form into balls, 1 1/2 inches in diameter. Dip each in remaining 1/4 cup melted butter and roll in cocoa-sugar mixture. Place balls in prepared pan. Bake 45 to 50 minutes or until golden brown. Cool 10 minutes in pan; invert onto serving plate. Serve warm or cool.   *12 servings*

Mini Chips Pancakes

*C*innamon Chip Muffins

- 2 cups all-purpose biscuit baking mix
- ¹/₄ cup sugar
- 1 egg
- ²/₃ cup milk
- 1 cup HERSHEY'S MINI CHIPS Semi-Sweet Chocolate
- ¹/₄ cup finely chopped nuts (optional)
  Sugar-Cinnamon Topping (recipe follows)

Heat oven to 400°. Grease or paper-line 12 muffin cups (2¹/₂ inches in diameter). In large bowl combine baking mix, sugar, egg and milk. Beat with spoon 30 seconds. Stir in MINI CHIPS Chocolate and nuts, if desired. Fill muffin cups ³/₄ full with batter. Sprinkle each with about ¹/₂ teaspoon Sugar-Cinnamon Topping. Bake 15 to 17 minutes or until very lightly browned. Serve warm. *About 1 dozen muffins*

Sugar-Cinnamon Topping

In small bowl combine 2 tablespoons sugar and 2 teaspoons ground cinnamon.

*M*ini Chips Pancakes 🍴 ⚾

- 1 carton (16 ounces) frozen pancake batter, thawed
- ¹/₂ cup HERSHEY'S MINI CHIPS Semi-Sweet Chocolate
  Fruit syrup or pancake syrup

Lightly grease griddle; heat to 375°. In small bowl combine pancake batter and MINI CHIPS Chocolate. Pour about 2 tablespoons batter onto hot griddle. Turn when surface is bubbly; cook until lightly browned. Serve warm with syrup. *About 14 four-inch pancakes*

Mini Chips Blueberry Bread ⬡

- 2 packages (14.5 ounces each)·blueberry nut quick bread mix
- 2 eggs, slightly beaten
- 3/4 cup buttermilk or sour milk*
- 1/2 cup vegetable oil
- 1 1/2 cups HERSHEY'S MINI CHIPS Semi-Sweet Chocolate
- MINI CHIPS Glaze (recipe follows)

Heat oven to 350°. Grease and flour 12-cup Bundt pan. In large bowl combine bread mix, eggs, buttermilk and oil. Beat with spoon 1 minute. Stir in MINI CHIPS Chocolate. Pour into prepared pan. Bake 45 to 50 minutes or until wooden pick inserted in center comes out clean. Cool 10 minutes; remove from pan. Wrap tightly in foil. Cool completely. Glaze with MINI CHIPS Glaze.   *12 servings*

*To sour milk: Use 2 teaspoons white vinegar plus milk to equal 3/4 cup.

Loaf Version: Prepare half of batter as directed above using 1 package blueberry nut quick bread mix, 1 egg, 6 tablespoons buttermilk or sour milk, 1/4 cup vegetable oil and 3/4 cup MINI CHIPS Semi-Sweet Chocolate. Pour batter into greased and floured 9 × 5 × 3-inch loaf pan. Bake; cool as directed above.   *1 loaf*

MINI CHIPS Glaze ✪

In small saucepan bring 2 tablespoons sugar and 2 tablespoons water to boil, stirring until sugar dissolves. Remove from heat; add 1/2 cup HERSHEY'S MINI CHIPS Semi-Sweet Chocolate. Stir with wire whisk until chips are melted and mixture is smooth; use immediately.

About 1/2 cup glaze

Mini Chips Blueberry Breakfast Cake ⬡

- 1 package (14.5 ounces) blueberry nut quick bread mix
- 1 cup dairy sour cream
- 1/4 cup water
- 1 egg
- 1/2 cup HERSHEY'S MINI CHIPS Semi-Sweet Chocolate
- Topping (recipe follows)

Heat oven to 350°. Grease bottom only of 9-inch square baking pan. In medium bowl combine bread mix, sour cream, water, egg and MINI CHIPS Chocolate; stir until well moistened and blended. Spread into prepared pan. Sprinkle Topping over batter. Bake 40 to 45 minutes or until golden brown. Cool; cut into squares.

9 servings

Topping

In small bowl combine 1/4 cup all-purpose flour, 1/4 cup sugar and 2 tablespoons softened butter or margarine until crumbly. Stir in 1/4 cup MINI CHIPS Chocolate.

Mini Chips Blueberry Bread (top) and Mini Chips Breakfast Cake (bottom)

Chocolate Chip Crater Cake ⓣ

- **2 cups all-purpose biscuit baking mix**
- **¹/₄ cup sugar**
- **²/₃ cup milk**
- **1 egg**
- **1 teaspoon vanilla extract**
- **1 cup HERSHEY'S Semi-Sweet Chocolate Chips**
- **Topping Mix (recipe follows)**

Heat oven to 350°. Grease 8-inch square baking pan. In large mixer bowl combine biscuit mix, sugar, milk, egg and vanilla; beat on low speed until moistened. Beat 2 minutes on medium speed until smooth. Pour ½ of batter into prepared pan. Sprinkle chocolate chips over batter. Top with remaining batter, completely covering chips. Sprinkle Topping Mix evenly over batter. Bake 25 to 30 minutes or until top springs back when touched lightly. Cool completely.   *About 9 servings*

Topping Mix

- **¹/₄ cup granulated sugar**
- **¹/₄ cup packed dark brown sugar**
- **¹/₄ cup packaged all-purpose biscuit baking mix**
- **¹/₄ cup butter or margarine, softened**
- **1 teaspoon ground cinnamon**

In small bowl combine all ingredients.

Chocolate Upside-Down Coffeecake Ⓣ

³/₄ cup apple jelly
1 package (16 ounces) pound cake mix
1 cup HERSHEY'S Milk Chocolate Chips, divided

Heat oven to 325°. Grease and flour 9-inch square baking pan. Spread jelly evenly onto bottom of prepared pan. Prepare cake batter according to package directions. Stir in ¹/₂ cup milk chocolate chips. Pour batter over jelly layer, spreading gently and evenly. Sprinkle remaining ¹/₂ cup chips over top. Bake 50 to 55 minutes or until cake springs back when touched lightly. Cool 5 minutes in pan; invert onto serving plate. Cool at least 15 minutes; serve warm. *About 9 servings*

Cocoa-Nut Bread

2¹/₄ cups all-purpose flour
1¹/₂ cups sugar
¹/₃ cup HERSHEY'S Cocoa
3¹/₂ teaspoons baking powder
1 teaspoon salt
1 egg
1¹/₄ cups milk
¹/₂ cup vegetable oil
1 cup finely chopped nuts

Heat oven to 350°. Grease and flour 9 x 5 x 3-inch loaf pan. In large bowl combine all ingredients except nuts. Beat with spoon 30 seconds; stir in nuts. Pour into prepared pan. Bake 65 to 70 minutes or until wooden pick inserted in center comes out clean. Cool 10 minutes; remove from pan. Wrap tightly in foil. Cool completely. *1 loaf*

Chocolate Almond Braided Coffeecake Ⓣ

¹/₃ cup HERSHEY'S Semi-Sweet Chocolate Chips, melted and cooled
¹/₃ cup sugar
¹/₄ cup dairy sour cream
2 tablespoons chopped, toasted almonds*
1 can (8 ounces) refrigerated quick crescent dinner rolls

Heat oven to 350°. In small mixer bowl combine melted chocolate, sugar and sour cream; stir in almonds. On ungreased cookie sheet unroll dough into 2 long rectangles. Overlap long sides to form 13 x 7-inch rectangle; press perforations to seal. Spread chocolate mixture in 2-inch strip lengthwise down center of dough. Make cuts 1 inch apart on each side just to edge of filling. Fold strips at an angle across filling, alternating from side to side. Fold under ends to seal. Bake 20 to 25 minutes or until browned. Cool; cut into slices. Serve warm.
8 servings

*To toast almonds: Toast in shallow baking pan in 350° oven, stirring occasionally, 8 to 10 minutes or until golden brown.

CANDIES & SNACKS

Easiest-ever candies for holiday gift giving, plus plenty of great treats for anytime snacking.

Clockwise from left: Easy Double Decker Fudge, Pastel-Coated Cocoa Bonbons, Easy Rocky Road (recipes page 54) and Coconut Honey Bars (recipe page 61)

53

*E*asy Rocky Road

2 cups (12-ounce package)
   HERSHEY'S Semi-Sweet
   Chocolate Chips
1/4 cup butter or margarine
2 tablespoons shortening
3 cups miniature
   marshmallows
1/2 cup coarsely chopped nuts

Butter 8-inch square pan. In large
microwave-safe bowl place
chocolate chips, butter and
shortening; microwave at MEDIUM
(50%) 5 to 7 minutes or until chips
are melted and mixture is smooth
when stirred. Add marshmallows
and nuts; blend well. Spread
evenly into prepared pan. Cover;
chill until firm. Cut into 2-inch
squares.   *16 squares*

*P*astel-Coated Cocoa Bonbons ◖

2 packages (3 ounces each)
   cream cheese, softened
2 cups confectioners' sugar
1/2 cup HERSHEY'S Cocoa
2 tablespoons butter, melted
1 teaspoon vanilla extract
   Pastel Coating (recipe
   follows)

In small mixer bowl beat cream
cheese. Add confectioners' sugar,
cocoa, butter and vanilla; blend
well. Cover; chill several hours or
until firm enough to handle.
Shape into 1-inch balls; place on
wax paper-covered tray. Chill,
uncovered, 3 to 4 hours or until
dry. Using long fork dip cold
centers into very warm Pastel

Coating. Quickly remove. Place
on wax paper-covered tray; swirl
coating on top of bonbon. Chill
until firm. Store in airtight
container in refrigerator.
                    2 dozen bonbons

Pastel Coating ◉

6 tablespoons butter
3 cups confectioners' sugar
1/4 cup milk
1 teaspoon vanilla extract
   Red or green food color

In medium microwave-safe bowl
combine all ingredients except
food color. Microwave at HIGH
(100%) 1 to 1 1/2 minutes or until
smooth when stirred. Tint pastel
pink or green with several drops
food color.

*E*asy Double Decker Fudge ◖◉

2 cups (12-ounce package)
   REESE'S Peanut Butter Chips
2 cups (12-ounce package)
   HERSHEY'S Semi-Sweet
   Chocolate Chips
2 cans (14 ounces each)
   sweetened condensed
   milk, divided
3 tablespoons butter

Line 13 x 9 x 2-inch pan with foil.
Place peanut butter chips and
chocolate chips in two separate
medium microwave-safe bowls.
Pour 1 can sweetened condensed
milk into each bowl. Microwave

bowl with peanut butter chips at HIGH (100%) 1½ to 2 minutes or until chips are melted and mixture is smooth when stirred; stir in butter. Immediately pour and spread into prepared pan. Microwave bowl with chocolate chips at HIGH 1½ to 2 minutes or until chips are melted and mixture is smooth when stirred. Immediately pour and spread over peanut butter layer. Cool. Cover; chill until firm. Cut into 1-inch squares.

About 8 dozen squares

*C*hocolate Marshmallow Slices ◗

2 cups (12-ounce package) HERSHEY'S Semi-Sweet Chocolate Chips
½ cup butter or margarine
6 cups (10½-ounce package) miniature marshmallows
1 cup finely chopped nuts
Additional chopped nuts

In medium saucepan over low heat melt chocolate chips and butter, stirring constantly until blended. Remove from heat; cool 5 minutes. Stir in marshmallows and 1 cup nuts; *do not melt marshmallows.* On wax paper shape mixture into 2 rolls, 2 inches in diameter. Wrap in foil; chill 15 minutes. Roll in additional chopped nuts. Wrap; chill overnight. Cut rolls into ¼-inch slices. Store in airtight container in cool, dry place.

About 3 dozen slices

Chocolate-Dipped Snacks

- ¹/₂ cup **HERSHEY'S** Milk Chocolate Chips
- ¹/₂ cup **HERSHEY'S** Semi-Sweet Chocolate Chips
- 1 tablespoon shortening
  Potato chips, cookies, dried apricots or miniature pretzels

In small microwave-safe bowl place milk chocolate chips, semi-sweet chocolate chips and shortening. Microwave at HIGH (100%) 1 to 1¹/₂ minutes or just until chips are melted and mixture is smooth when stirred. Cool slightly. Dip ²/₃ of each snack or fruit into chocolate mixture. Shake gently to remove excess chocolate. Place on wax paper-covered tray. Chill, uncovered, about 30 minutes or until chocolate is firm. Store in airtight container in cool, dry place.   *About ¹/₂ cup coating*

Chocolate-Peanut Butter Clusters

- ¹/₂ cup **HERSHEY'S** Milk Chocolate Chips
- ¹/₂ cup **HERSHEY'S** Semi-Sweet Chocolate Chips
- 1 tablespoon shortening
- 1 cup unsalted, roasted peanuts

In small microwave-safe bowl place milk chocolate chips, semi-sweet chocolate chips and shortening. Microwave at HIGH (100%) 1 to 1¹/₂ minutes or just until chips are melted and mixture is smooth when stirred. Stir in peanuts. Drop by teaspoonfuls into 1-inch diameter candy or petit four papers. Allow to set until firm. Store in airtight container in cool, dry place.

About 2 dozen clusters

Chocolate-Dipped Snacks

Cocoa Fruit Balls ◗

2½ cups (about 12 ounces)
    mixed dried fruits (prunes,
    pears, apricots and
    apples)
1¼ cups (8 ounces) Mission figs
  1 cup flaked coconut
  2 tablespoons orange juice
  2 tablespoons honey
  ½ cup HERSHEY'S Cocoa
    Chopped nuts or
    confectioners' sugar

Remove pits from prunes and stems from figs, if necessary. Using metal blade of food processor, chop dried fruits, figs and coconut (or put through fine blade of food grinder). In large bowl combine orange juice, honey and cocoa with fruit-coconut mixture; mix well. Cover; chill thoroughly. Shape mixture into 1¼-inch balls. Roll in chopped nuts or confectioners' sugar. Store in airtight container at room temperature.

About 3 dozen balls

Chocolate Almond Logs ◗

  1 can (8 ounces) almond
    paste
  2 cups vanilla wafer cookie
    crumbs (about 60 cookies,
    crushed)
1⅓ cups confectioners' sugar
  1 cup HERSHEY'S Cocoa
  1 cup whipping cream
1½ cups finely chopped
    almonds
    Candied cherries, cut in half

In large bowl crumble almond paste with pastry blender. Combine vanilla wafer crumbs, confectioners' sugar and cocoa; add to almond paste. Stir in whipping cream; mix until well blended. Knead and shape mixture into smooth ball. Shape mixture into 2 rolls, 2 inches in diameter; roll in chopped almonds. Wrap in foil; chill until firm. Cut rolls into ¼-inch slices; garnish with candied cherry halves. Store in airtight container in cool, dry place.

About 6 dozen slices

Note: Can be made entirely in food processor. Chop cookies and nuts separately; combine and add ingredients as directed.

Mint 'n Chocolate Fudge

½ cup butter or margarine
¾ cup HERSHEY'S Cocoa
4 cups confectioners' sugar
1 teaspoon vanilla extract
½ cup evaporated milk
Pastel Mint Topping (recipe follows)

Line 8-inch square pan with foil. In medium microwave-safe bowl place butter. Microwave at HIGH (100%) 1 to 1½ minutes or until melted. Add cocoa; stir until smooth. Stir in confectioners' sugar and vanilla; blend well (mixture will be dry and crumbly). Stir in evaporated milk. Microwave at HIGH 1 to 2 minutes or until mixture is hot. Beat with whisk until smooth. Immediately pour into prepared pan. Cover; chill until firm. Spread Pastel Mint Topping evenly over fudge; chill until firm. Cut into 1-inch squares. Cover; store in refrigerator.

About 4 dozen squares

Pastel Mint Topping

In small mixer bowl beat 3 tablespoons softened butter or margarine, 1 tablespoon water and ⅛ to ¼ teaspoon mint extract until blended. Gradually add 1½ cups confectioners' sugar and 2 drops green or red food color. Beat until smooth.

Fast Chocolate-Pecan Fudge

½ cup butter or margarine
¾ cup HERSHEY'S Cocoa
4 cups confectioners' sugar
1 teaspoon vanilla extract
½ cup evaporated milk
1 cup pecan pieces
Pecan halves (optional)

Line 8-inch square pan with foil. In medium microwave-safe bowl place butter. Microwave at HIGH (100%) 1 to 1½ minutes or until melted. Add cocoa; stir until smooth. Stir in confectioners' sugar and vanilla; blend well (mixture will be dry and crumbly). Stir in evaporated milk. Microwave at HIGH 1 minute; stir. Microwave additional 1 minute or until mixture is hot. Beat with wooden spoon until smooth; add pecan pieces. Pour into prepared pan. Cool. Cover; chill until firm. Cut into 1-inch squares. Garnish with pecan halves, if desired. Cover; store in refrigerator.

About 4 dozen squares

Conventional Directions:
Prepare pan as above. In medium saucepan melt butter. Remove from heat; stir in cocoa. Stir in confectioners' sugar and vanilla; add evaporated milk. Stir constantly over low heat until warm and smooth; add pecan pieces. Pour into prepared pan; chill and store as above.

From top to bottom: Cherries 'n Chocolate Fudge (recipe page 61), Fast Chocolate-Pecan Fudge and Mint 'n Chocolate Fudge

Rich 'n Good Chocolate Truffles ◖

1 2/3 cups whipping cream
1/2 cup butter or margarine
1 box (8 ounces) HERSHEY'S Semi-Sweet Baking Chocolate, broken into pieces and chopped*
1 1/3 cups HERSHEY'S Semi-Sweet Chocolate Chips, chopped*
1 tablespoon vanilla extract or desired liqueur
Coating (recipe follows)

In medium saucepan combine whipping cream and butter. Cook over medium heat, stirring constantly, just until mixture boils; remove from heat. Stir in baking chocolate and chocolate chips until completely melted; continue stirring until mixture cools and thickens slightly. Stir in vanilla. Pour into shallow glass dish. Cover; chill until firm. With spoon scoop mixture into 1-inch balls; roll in Coating. Cover; chill until firm. Reroll before serving, if desired. Serve cold.

About 4 dozen truffles

Coating
In small bowl combine 1/2 cup HERSHEY'S Cocoa, sifted, and 3 tablespoons confectioners' sugar, sifted.

*Food processor can be used for chopping chocolate.

Rich 'n Good Chocolate Truffles (top) and Mocha Truffles (bottom)

Mocha Truffles ◖

- ¼ cup whipping cream
- 3 tablespoons sugar
- 3 tablespoons butter
- 1½ teaspoons powdered instant coffee
- ½ cup HERSHEY'S Semi-Sweet Chocolate Chips
- ½ teaspoon vanilla extract
  Chopped nuts or HERSHEY'S Semi-Sweet Baking Chocolate, grated

In small saucepan combine whipping cream, sugar, butter and instant coffee; cook over low heat, stirring constantly, just until mixture boils. Remove from heat; immediately add chocolate chips. Stir until chips are melted and mixture is smooth when stirred; add vanilla. Pour into small bowl; chill, stirring occasionally, until mixture begins to set. Cover; chill several hours or overnight to allow mixture to ripen and harden. Form small amounts of mixture into ½-inch balls, working quickly to prevent melting; roll in nuts or chocolate. Cover; store in refrigerator. Serve cold.

About 1½ dozen truffles

Cherries 'n Chocolate Fudge ◉ ◖

- 1 can (14 ounces) sweetened condensed milk
- 2 cups (12-ounce package) HERSHEY'S Semi-Sweet Chocolate Chips
- ½ cup coarsely chopped almonds
- ½ cup chopped candied cherries
- 1 teaspoon almond extract
  Candied cherry halves (optional)

Line 8-inch square pan with foil. In medium microwave-safe bowl combine sweetened condensed milk and chocolate chips; stir lightly. Microwave at HIGH (100%) 1½ to 2 minutes or until chips are melted and mixture is smooth when stirred. Stir in almonds, cherries and almond extract. Spread evenly in prepared pan. Cover; chill until firm. Cut into 1-inch squares. Garnish with cherry halves, if desired. Cover; store in refrigerator.

About 4 dozen squares

Coconut Honey Bars

- ⅓ cup butter or margarine
- ⅓ cup packed light brown sugar
- ⅓ cup honey
- ½ teaspoon vanilla extract
- 2 cups quick-cooking rolled oats
- 1⅓ cups flaked coconut
- ½ cup raisins
- 1 cup REESE'S Peanut Butter Chips or HERSHEY'S Semi-Sweet Chocolate Chips

Heat oven to 400°. Grease 8-inch square baking pan. In large saucepan melt butter; remove from heat. Add remaining ingredients; stir until blended. Press mixture into prepared pan. Bake 15 to 20 minutes or just until golden brown. Cool completely; cut into bars.

About 2 dozen bars

CHEESECAKES

A variety of luscious cheesecake creations to choose from.

Clockwise from top: Simple Chocolate Cheesecakes, Black-Eyed Susan Cheesecakes (recipes page 64) and Individual Mocha Cheesecakes (recipe page 68)

Simple Chocolate Cheesecakes ◖

24 vanilla wafer cookies
2 packages (8 ounces each) cream cheese, softened
1¼ cups sugar
⅓ cup HERSHEY'S Cocoa
2 tablespoons all-purpose flour
3 eggs
1 cup dairy sour cream
1 teaspoon vanilla extract
Sour Cream Topping (recipe follows)
Canned cherry pie filling, chilled

Heat oven to 350°. Line muffin pans with foil-laminated paper bake cups (2½ inches in diameter). Place one vanilla wafer in bottom of each cup. In large mixer bowl beat cream cheese and sugar. Blend in cocoa and flour. Add eggs; beat well. Blend in sour cream and vanilla. Fill each prepared cup almost full with cheese mixture. Bake 15 to 20 minutes or just until set. Remove from oven; cool 5 to 10 minutes. Spread heaping teaspoonful Sour Cream Topping on surface of each cup. Cool completely; chill. Garnish with cherry pie filling just before serving.
About 2 dozen cheesecakes

Sour Cream Topping
In small bowl combine 1 cup dairy sour cream, 2 tablespoons sugar and 1 teaspoon vanilla extract; stir until sugar dissolves.

Black-Eyed Susan Cheesecakes ◖

24 vanilla wafer cookies
2 packages (8 ounces each) cream cheese, softened
½ cup sugar
2 eggs
½ teaspoon vanilla extract
1 cup REESE'S Peanut Butter Chips
½ cup HERSHEY'S Semi-Sweet Chocolate Chips
3 tablespoons butter or margarine

Heat oven to 350°. Line muffin pans with foil-laminated paper bake cups (2 inches in diameter). Place one vanilla wafer in bottom of each cup. In large mixer bowl beat cream cheese and sugar. Add eggs and vanilla; beat well. Stir in peanut butter chips. Spoon 1 heaping tablespoon cheese mixture into each cup. Bake 15 minutes or just until set, but not browned. Cool. In small microwave-safe bowl place chocolate chips and butter. Microwave at HIGH (100%) 30 seconds to 1 minute or until chips are melted and mixture is smooth when stirred. Drop teaspoonfuls of chocolate mixture onto center of each cheesecake, letting white show around edge. Garnish as desired. Cover; chill.
About 2 dozen cheesecakes

No-Bake Chocolate Cheesecake

1½ cups HERSHEY'S Semi-Sweet Chocolate Chips
1 package (8 ounces) cream cheese, softened
1 package (3 ounces) cream cheese, softened
½ cup sugar
¼ cup butter or margarine, softened
2 cups frozen non-dairy whipped topping, thawed
8-inch (6 ounces) packaged graham cracker crumb crust

In small microwave-safe bowl place chocolate chips. Microwave at HIGH (100%) 1 to 1½ minutes or until chips are melted and mixture is smooth when stirred. Set aside to cool. In large mixer bowl beat cream cheese, sugar and butter until smooth. On low speed blend in melted chocolate. Fold in whipped topping until blended. Spoon cheese mixture into crust. Cover; chill until firm. Garnish as desired.

About 8 servings

Chocolate Swirl Cheesecake

- **4 packages (3 ounces each) cream cheese, softened**
- **1/2 cup sugar**
- **2 eggs**
- **2 teaspoons vanilla extract**
- **1/2 cup HERSHEY'S Semi-Sweet Chocolate Chips or MINI CHIPS Semi-Sweet Chocolate**
- **1 teaspoon shortening**
- **8-inch (6 ounces) packaged graham cracker crumb crust**

Heat oven to 325°. In large mixer bowl beat cream cheese and sugar. Add eggs and vanilla; beat well. In small bowl reserve 1/2 cup cream cheese mixture. Melt chocolate chips with shortening in top of double boiler over hot, not boiling, water; stir into reserved 1/2 cup cream cheese mixture. Pour vanilla mixture into crust. Spoon chocolate mixture by dollops onto vanilla mixture. Using tip of knife swirl for marbled effect. Place filled crust on cookie sheet. Bake 25 to 30 minutes or until center is almost set. Cool on wire rack. Cover; chill several hours or until firm. Garnish as desired.

8 servings

Elegant Peanut Butter Cheesecake ◐

- 8-inch (6 ounces) packaged chocolate flavored crumb crust
- 1/4 cup HERSHEY'S Semi-Sweet Chocolate Chips
- 2 cups (12-ounce package) REESE'S Peanut Butter Chips
- 1 package (8 ounces) cream cheese, softened
- 1/2 cup packed light brown sugar
- 3 egg yolks
- 1 cup chilled whipping cream
- 3/4 cup chopped unsalted, roasted peanuts, divided

Heat oven to 350°. Heat crust in oven 5 minutes. Remove from oven; sprinkle chocolate chips in bottom of crust. When chips melt, spread over bottom of crust. Chill crust 5 to 10 minutes or until chocolate hardens. In top of double boiler over hot, not boiling, water melt peanut butter chips, stirring constantly to blend; cool slightly. In large mixer bowl beat cream cheese, melted peanut butter chips, brown sugar and egg yolks until smooth. In small mixer bowl beat whipping cream until stiff. Fold whipped cream and 1/2 cup peanuts into cream cheese mixture; spoon into crust. Sprinkle remaining 1/4 cup peanuts over top. Cover; chill until firm. Garnish as desired.

8 servings

Individual Cocoa Cheesecakes 🌑 Ⓝ

⅓ cup graham cracker crumbs
⅓ cup plus 1 tablespoon sugar, divided
1 tablespoon butter or margarine, melted
1 package (8 ounces) cream cheese, softened
3 tablespoons HERSHEY'S Cocoa
1 teaspoon vanilla extract
1 tablespoon milk
1 egg

In small bowl combine graham cracker crumbs, 1 tablespoon sugar and butter. Press about 1 tablespoon crumb mixture onto bottom of 6 microwave-safe ramekins (2½ to 3 inches in diameter). In small mixer bowl beat cream cheese, remaining ⅓ cup sugar, cocoa and vanilla. Add milk and egg, beating just until smooth and well blended. Divide cheese mixture evenly among ramekins, filling each to ¼ inch from top. Microwave at MEDIUM-HIGH (70%) 2 minutes, rotating dishes after 1 minute. Microwave at HIGH (100%) 30 to 40 seconds or until puffed in center. Cool; chill before serving. Garnish as desired.   6 cheesecakes

Note: Substitute paper-lined microwave-safe muffin cups (2½ inches in diameter) for ramekins, if desired.

Cocoa Cheesecake 🌑

Graham Crust (recipe follows)
2 packages (8 ounces each) cream cheese, softened
¾ cup plus 2 tablespoons sugar, divided
½ cup HERSHEY'S Cocoa
2 teaspoons vanilla extract, divided
2 eggs
1 cup dairy sour cream

Prepare Graham Crust; set aside. Heat oven to 375°. In large mixer bowl beat cream cheese, ¾ cup sugar, cocoa and 1 teaspoon vanilla until light and fluffy. Add eggs; blend well. Pour cheese mixture into prepared crust. Bake 20 minutes. Remove from oven; cool 15 minutes. Increase oven temperature to 425°. In small bowl, combine sour cream, remaining 2 tablespoons sugar and remaining 1 teaspoon vanilla; stir until smooth. Spread evenly over baked filling. Bake 10 minutes. Cool; chill several hours or overnight.   *10 to 12 servings*

Graham Crust 🅧
In small bowl, combine 1½ cups graham cracker crumbs, ⅓ cup sugar and ⅓ cup melted butter or margarine. Press mixture onto bottom and halfway up side of 9-inch springform pan.

Chocolate Lover's Cheesecake: Prepare as above, adding 1 cup HERSHEY'S Semi-Sweet Chocolate Chips after eggs have been blended into mixture. Bake and serve as directed.

Mocha Cheesecake

Chocolate Cookie Crust
(recipe follows)
4 packages (3 ounces each)
cream cheese, softened
2½ tablespoons butter or
margarine, softened
1 cup sugar
2 eggs
5 tablespoons HERSHEY'S
Cocoa
¾ teaspoon vanilla extract
1 tablespoon powdered
instant coffee
1 teaspoon boiling water
1 cup dairy sour cream

Prepare Chocolate Cookie Crust;
set aside. Heat oven to 325°. In
large mixer bowl beat cream
cheese and butter until smooth
and fluffy. Gradually beat in sugar.
Add eggs, one at a time, beating
well after each addition. Beat in
cocoa and vanilla. Dissolve instant
coffee in water; stir into cheese
mixture. Add sour cream; blend
well. Pour cheese mixture into
pan. Bake 30 minutes. Turn off
oven; leave cheesecake in oven
15 minutes without opening door.
Remove from oven. Cool in pan
on wire rack. Cover; chill. Garnish
as desired. *10 to 12 servings*

Chocolate Cookie Crust

22 chocolate wafers (½ of 8½-
ounce package)
¼ cup cold butter or
margarine, cut into ½-inch
slices
⅛ teaspoon ground cinnamon

Crush wafers in food processor or
blender to form fine crumbs. In
medium bowl mix crumbs, butter
and cinnamon until evenly
blended. Press mixture evenly on
bottom of 9-inch springform pan.

COOKIES & COOKIE BARS

Here's all kinds of cookies to choose from— all made delicious with chocolate.

From top to bottom: Hershey's Great American Chocolate Chip Cookies (recipe page 72) and Reese's™ Chewy Chocolate Cookies (recipe page 86).

Hershey's Great American Chocolate Chip Cookies

1 cup butter, softened
3/4 cup granulated sugar
3/4 cup packed light brown sugar
1 teaspoon vanilla extract
2 eggs
2 1/4 cups all-purpose flour
1 teaspoon baking soda
1/2 teaspoon salt
2 cups (12-ounce package) HERSHEY'S Semi-Sweet Chocolate Chips
1 cup chopped nuts (optional)

Heat oven to 375°. In large mixer bowl cream butter, granulated sugar, brown sugar and vanilla until light and fluffy. Add eggs; beat well. Combine flour, baking soda and salt; gradually blend into creamed mixture. Stir in chocolate chips and nuts, if desired. Drop by rounded teaspoonfuls onto ungreased cookie sheet. Bake 8 to 10 minutes or until very lightly browned. Cool slightly; remove from cookie sheet to wire rack. Cool completely.

About 6 dozen cookies

Pan Recipe: Spread batter in greased 15 1/2 x 10 1/2 x 1-inch jelly-roll pan. Bake at 375° for 20 minutes or until lightly browned. Cool completely. Cut into bars.

About 4 dozen bars

Double Fudge Saucepan Brownies

1/2 cup sugar
2 tablespoons butter or margarine
2 tablespoons water
2 cups (12-ounce package) HERSHEY'S Semi-Sweet Chocolate Chips, divided
2 eggs, slightly beaten
1 teaspoon vanilla extract
2/3 cup all-purpose flour
1/4 teaspoon baking soda
1/4 teaspoon salt
1/2 cup chopped nuts (optional)

Heat oven to 325°. Grease 9-inch square baking pan. In medium saucepan over low heat cook sugar, butter and water, stirring constantly, until mixture comes to boil. Remove from heat; immediately add 1 cup chocolate chips, stirring until chips are melted. Stir in eggs and vanilla until blended. Combine flour, baking soda and salt; stir into chocolate mixture. Stir in remaining 1 cup chips and nuts, if desired. Pour into prepared pan. Bake 25 to 30 minutes or until brownies begin to pull away from sides of pan. Cool completely. Cut into bars.

About 1 1/2 dozen brownies

Reese's™ Cookies

- 1 cup shortening OR ³/₄ cup butter or margarine
- 1 cup granulated sugar
- ¹/₂ cup packed light brown sugar
- 1 teaspoon vanilla extract
- 2 eggs
- 2 cups all-purpose flour
- 1 teaspoon baking soda
- 1 cup REESE'S Peanut Butter Chips
- 1 cup HERSHEY'S Semi-Sweet or Milk Chocolate Chips

Heat oven to 350°. In large mixer bowl cream shortening or butter, granulated sugar, brown sugar and vanilla. Add eggs; beat well. Combine flour and baking soda; blend into creamed mixture. Stir in peanut butter chips and chocolate chips. Drop by rounded teaspoonfuls onto ungreased cookie sheet. Bake 10 to 12 minutes or until very lightly browned. Cool slightly; remove from cookie sheet to wire rack. Cool completely.

About 5 dozen cookies

Peanut Butter Chips and Jelly Bars

- 1¹/₂ cups all-purpose flour
- ¹/₂ cup sugar
- ³/₄ teaspoon baking powder
- ¹/₂ cup butter or margarine
- 1 egg, beaten
- ³/₄ cup grape jelly
- 1 cup REESE'S Peanut Butter Chips, divided

Heat oven to 375°. Grease 9-inch square baking pan. In medium bowl combine flour, sugar and baking powder; cut in butter with pastry blender or fork to form coarse crumbs. Add egg; blend well. Reserve half of mixture; press remaining mixture onto bottom of prepared pan. Spread jelly evenly over crust. Sprinkle ¹/₂ cup peanut butter chips over jelly. Combine remaining crumb mixture with remaining ¹/₂ cup chips; sprinkle over top. Bake 25 to 30 minutes or until lightly browned. Cool completely. Cut into bars.

About 1¹/₂ dozen bars

Peanut Butter Chips and Jelly Bars

Cherry Cordial Cookies 🔲

> 1 package (18.25 ounces) cherry cake mix
> ³/₄ cup butter or margarine, softened
> 2 eggs
> 1 cup HERSHEY'S MINI CHIPS Semi-Sweet Chocolate
> MINI CHIPS Glaze (recipe follows)

Heat oven to 350°. In large mixer bowl combine cake mix, butter and eggs; mix well. Stir in MINI CHIPS Chocolate. Drop by rounded teaspoonfuls onto ungreased cookie sheet. Bake 10 to 12 minutes or until almost set. Cool slightly; remove from cookie sheet to wire rack. Cool completely. Drizzle MINI CHIPS Glaze onto cooled cookies; allow to set.   *About 4 dozen cookies*

Mini Chips Glaze 🌐 ⚙
In small microwave-safe bowl place 1 cup HERSHEY'S MINI CHIPS Semi-Sweet Chocolate and 3 tablespoons shortening (not butter, margarine or oil). Microwave at HIGH (100%) 45 seconds; stir. If necessary, microwave at HIGH additional 15 seconds or until melted and smooth when stirred. Use immediately.

Double Chocolate Black-Eyed Susans

1 package (18.25 or 19.75 ounces) fudge marble cake mix
1 egg
1/3 cup vegetable oil
4 tablespoons water, divided
1 cup HERSHEY'S MINI CHIPS Semi-Sweet Chocolate

Heat oven to 350°. In large bowl combine cake mix, egg, oil and 3 tablespoons water; mix with spoon until thoroughly blended. Stir in MINI CHIPS Chocolate. In small bowl combine 2/3 cup batter, chocolate packet from cake mix and remaining 1 tablespoon water; mix well. Drop vanilla batter by rounded teaspoonfuls onto lightly greased cookie sheet; press thumb or back of spoon gently in center of each cookie. Drop chocolate batter by rounded half-teaspoonfuls onto top of each cookie. Bake 10 to 12 minutes or until very lightly browned. Cool slightly; remove from cookie sheet to wire rack. Cool completely.
About 3 dozen cookies

English Toffee Bars

English Toffee Bars

2 cups all-purpose flour
1 cup packed light brown
   sugar
1/2 cup butter
1 cup pecan halves
   Toffee Topping (recipe
   follows)
1 cup HERSHEY'S Milk
   Chocolate Chips

Heat oven to 350°. In large mixer bowl combine flour, brown sugar and butter; mix until fine crumbs form. (A few large crumbs may remain.) Press into ungreased 13 × 9 × 2-inch baking pan. Sprinkle pecans over crust. Drizzle Toffee Topping evenly over pecans and crust. Bake 20 to 22 minutes or until topping is bubbly and golden. Remove from oven. Immediately sprinkle chocolate chips over top; press gently onto surface. Cool completely. Cut into bars.   *About 3 dozen bars*

Toffee Topping
In small saucepan combine 2/3 cup butter and 1/3 cup packed light brown sugar. Cook over medium heat, stirring constantly, until mixture comes to boil; boil and stir 30 seconds. Use immediately.

Butter Pecan Squares

1/2 cup butter, softened
1/2 cup packed light brown
   sugar
1 egg
1 teaspoon vanilla extract
3/4 cup all-purpose flour
2 cups HERSHEY'S Milk
   Chocolate Chips, divided
3/4 cup chopped pecans,
   divided

Heat oven to 350°. Grease 8- or 9-inch square baking pan. In small mixer bowl cream butter, sugar, egg and vanilla until light and fluffy. Blend in flour. Stir in 1 cup chocolate chips and 1/2 cup pecans. Spread into prepared pan. Bake 25 to 30 minutes or until lightly browned. Remove from oven. Immediately sprinkle remaining 1 cup chips over surface. Let stand 5 to 10 minutes or until chips soften; spread evenly. Immediately sprinkle remaining 1/4 cup pecans over top; press gently onto chocolate. Cool completely. Cut into squares.
            About 16 squares

Butter Pecan Squares

_Drizzle-Topped
Brownies_

Drizzle-Topped Brownies ⬚

1¼ cups all-purpose biscuit
   baking mix
1 cup sugar
½ cup HERSHEY'S Cocoa
½ cup butter or margarine,
   melted
2 eggs
1 teaspoon vanilla extract
1 cup HERSHEY'S Semi-Sweet
   Chocolate Chips or MINI
   CHIPS
   Quick Vanilla Glaze (recipe
   follows)

Heat oven to 350°. Grease 8- or
9-inch square baking pan. In
medium bowl combine baking
mix, sugar and cocoa; mix with
spoon or fork until thoroughly
blended. Add butter, eggs and
vanilla, mixing well. Stir in
chocolate chips. Spread into
prepared pan. Bake 25 to 30
minutes or until wooden pick
inserted in center comes out
clean. Cool completely. Drizzle
Quick Vanilla Glaze over cooled
brownies. Cut into bars.
                    About 20 brownies

Quick Vanilla Glaze 🌀

In small bowl combine ½ cup
confectioners' sugar, 1 tablespoon
water and ¼ teaspoon vanilla
extract; blend well.

Luscious Layered Bars ⬚

½ cup butter or margarine
1 package (18.25 or 18.5
   ounces) chocolate cake
   mix
1 cup HERSHEY'S Semi-Sweet
   Chocolate Chips
1 cup REESE'S Peanut Butter
   Chips
1 cup shredded coconut
1 cup coarsely chopped
   walnuts or pecans
1 can (14 ounces) sweetened
   condensed milk

Heat oven to 325°. Grease
15½ × 10½ × 1-inch jelly-roll pan.
Cut butter into cake mix with
pastry blender or fork to form
coarse crumbs; sprinkle evenly in
prepared pan. Sprinkle chocolate
chips, peanut butter chips,
coconut and nuts over crumb
mixture. Drizzle sweetened
condensed milk evenly over top.
Bake 30 to 35 minutes or until
slightly bubbly and very lightly
browned. Cool completely. Cut
into bars.   _About 4 dozen bars_

Easy Peanutty Snickerdoodles

2 tablespoons sugar
2 teaspoons ground cinnamon
1 package (15 ounces) golden sugar cookie mix
1 egg
1 tablespoon water
1 cup REESE'S Peanut Butter Chips

Heat oven to 375°. In small bowl combine sugar and cinnamon. In medium bowl combine cookie mix (and enclosed flavor packet), egg and water; mix with spoon or fork until thoroughly blended. Stir in peanut butter chips. Shape dough into 1-inch balls. (If dough is too soft, cover and chill about 1 hour.) Roll balls in cinnamon-sugar. Place on ungreased cookie sheet. Bake 8 to 10 minutes or until very lightly browned. Cool slightly; remove from cookie sheet to wire rack. Cool completely.

About 2 dozen cookies

Chocolate Chip 'n Oatmeal Cookies

1 package (18.25 or 18.5 ounces) yellow cake mix
1 cup quick-cooking rolled oats
3/4 cup butter or margarine, softened
2 eggs
1 cup HERSHEY'S Semi-Sweet Chocolate Chips

Heat oven to 350°. In large mixer bowl combine cake mix, oats, butter and eggs; mix well. Stir in chocolate chips. Drop by rounded teaspoonfuls onto ungreased cookie sheet. Bake 10 to 12 minutes or until very lightly browned. Cool slightly; remove from cookie sheet to wire rack. Cool completely.

About 4 dozen cookies

Chocolate Kiss Cookies

1 package (15 ounces) golden sugar cookie mix
1/2 cup HERSHEY'S Cocoa
1 egg
2 tablespoons water
3/4 cup finely chopped nuts
1 bag (9 ounces) HERSHEY'S KISSES Chocolates, unwrapped (about 42)

Heat oven to 350°. In medium bowl combine cookie mix (and enclosed flavor packet), cocoa, egg and water; mix with spoon or fork until thoroughly blended. Shape dough into 1-inch balls. Roll balls in nuts; place on ungreased cookie sheet. Bake 8 minutes. Immediately press KISS into center of each warm cookie, allowing cookie to crack slightly. Cool slightly; remove from cookie sheet to wire rack. Cool completely.

About 3 1/2 dozen cookies

From top to bottom: Chocolate Chip 'n Oatmeal Cookies, Easy Peanutty Snickerdoodles and Chocolate Kiss Cookies

Reese's™ Chewy Chocolate Cookies

1¼ cups butter or margarine, softened
2 cups sugar
2 eggs
2 teaspoons vanilla extract
2 cups all-purpose flour
¾ cup HERSHEY'S Cocoa
1 teaspoon baking soda
½ teaspoon salt
2 cups (12-ounce package) REESE'S Peanut Butter Chips
½ cup finely chopped nuts (optional)

Heat oven to 350°. In large mixer bowl cream butter and sugar until light and fluffy. Add eggs and vanilla; beat well. Combine flour, cocoa, baking soda and salt; gradually blend into creamed mixture. Stir in peanut butter chips and nuts, if desired. Drop by teaspoonfuls onto ungreased cookie sheet. Bake 8 to 9 minutes.

(Do not overbake; cookies will be soft. They will puff while baking and flatten while cooling). Cool slightly; remove from cookie sheet to wire rack. Cool completely.
About 4½ dozen cookies

Peanut Butter Glazed Chocolate Cookies ⊕

1 package (15 ounces) golden sugar cookie mix
½ cup HERSHEY'S Cocoa
1 egg
2 tablespoons water
About 2 cups pecan halves
Peanut Butter Glaze (recipe follows)

Heat oven to 350°. In medium bowl combine cookie mix (and enclosed flavor packet), cocoa, egg and water; mix with spoon or fork until thoroughly blended. To form base for cookies, on cookie sheet, arrange 3 pecan halves with tips touching in center. Repeat for each cookie. Shape dough into 1-inch balls; gently

Peanut Butter Glazed Chocolate Cookies

press one ball onto each pecan cluster until pecans adhere. Bake 8 to 10 minutes or until *almost* set; *do not overbake*. Cool slightly; remove from cookie sheet to wire rack. Cool completely. Place wax paper or foil under rack of cookies. Gently spoon or drizzle thin coating of Peanut Butter Glaze onto each cookie. Allow glaze to set.

About 3½ dozen cookies

Peanut Butter Glaze 😊 Ⓝ

In top of double boiler over hot, not boiling, water melt 1 cup REESE'S Peanut Butter Chips and 2 tablespoons shortening (not butter, margarine or oil), stirring constantly to blend; remove from heat and use immediately. OR in small microwave-safe bowl place peanut chips with shortening. Microwave at HIGH (100%) 45 seconds; stir. If necessary, microwave at HIGH additional 15 seconds or until melted and smooth when stirred. Use immediately.

Signature Brownies

Signature Brownies Ⓣ

- 1 package (15 ounces) golden sugar cookie mix
- ½ cup HERSHEY'S Cocoa
- ½ cup HERSHEY'S Syrup
- ¼ cup butter or margarine, melted
- 1 egg
- ½ cup coarsely chopped nuts
  No-Cook Fudge Frosting (recipe follows)

Heat oven to 350°. Grease 8- or 9-inch square baking pan. In medium bowl combine cookie mix (and enclosed flavor packet) and cocoa. Stir in syrup, butter and egg, blending well. Stir in nuts. Spread into prepared pan. Bake 25 to 30 minutes or until wooden pick inserted in center comes out clean. Cool completely. Frost with No-Cook Fudge Frosting. Cut into bars.

About 20 brownies

No-Cook Fudge Frosting 😊

In small bowl combine 2 cups confectioners' sugar, ½ cup HERSHEY'S Syrup, ¼ cup HERSHEY'S Cocoa, ¼ cup melted butter or margarine and ½ teaspoon vanilla extract; blend well. Use immediately.

BEVERAGES

Rich cocoas to warm
you in winter, plus
frothy favorites to cool
you off in summer.

From left to right: Cocoa Fruit Breakfast Drink
(recipe page 84), Chocolate Shake and Double
Chocolate Malt (recipes page 85)

Spiced Mocha Mix ☻

- 1 cup sugar
- 1 cup nonfat dry milk powder
- 1/2 cup powdered non-dairy creamer
- 1/2 cup HERSHEY'S Cocoa
- 3 tablespoons powdered instant coffee
- 1/2 teaspoon ground allspice
- 1/4 teaspoon ground cinnamon
  Dash salt

In large bowl combine all ingredients. Store in airtight container.
2 1/2 cups mix (12 to 14 servings)

For Single Serving: Place 3 tablespoons mix in mug or cup; add 3/4 cup boiling water. Stir until mix is dissolved. Top with marshmallows, if desired. Serve immediately.

Quick Blender Hot Chocolate ☻

- 3 cups milk, heated to boiling
- 1 cup HERSHEY'S MINI CHIPS Semi-Sweet Chocolate

In blender container place milk and MINI CHIPS Chocolate. Cover; blend until smooth. Serve immediately.
About four 6-ounce servings

Cocoa Fruit Breakfast Drink ☻

- 1 container (8 ounces) strawberry yogurt
- 1 1/4 cups cold milk
- 1 cup fresh strawberries, sliced
- 1 ripe, medium banana, sliced
- 3 tablespoons HERSHEY'S Cocoa
- 2 tablespoons honey

In blender container place all ingredients. Cover; blend until smooth.
About five 6-ounce servings

Double Chocolate Malt

- 1/2 cup cold milk
- 1/4 cup HERSHEY'S Syrup
- 2 tablespoons chocolate malted milk powder
- 2 cups vanilla ice cream, softened

In blender container place milk, syrup and malted milk powder. Cover; blend. Add ice cream. Cover; blend until smooth. Serve immediately.

About three 6-ounce servings

VARIATION
Triple Chocolate Malt: Substitute chocolate ice cream for vanilla ice cream.

Chocolate Ice Cream Soda

- 3 tablespoons HERSHEY'S Syrup
- 1/4 cup cold ginger ale or club soda, freshly opened
- 2 scoops vanilla ice cream
  Additional cold ginger ale or club soda

In 12-ounce glass stir together syrup and 1/4 cup ginger ale. Add ice cream. Fill glass with additional ginger ale. Serve immediately.

1 soda

Chocolate Shake

- 2 cups cold milk
- 2 cups vanilla ice cream, divided
- 3/4 cup HERSHEY'S Syrup

In blender container place milk, 1 cup ice cream and syrup. Cover; blend until smooth. Pour into glasses; top with scoops of remaining ice cream.

About three 10-ounce servings

VARIATIONS
Before blending, add one of the following:

- 1 ripe, medium banana, sliced
- 2/3 cup drained, canned peach slices
- 1/2 teaspoon mint extract
- 1/2 cup crushed, sweetened strawberries

Choco Peanut Butter Shake

- 3/4 cup cold milk
- 1/4 cup creamy peanut butter
- 3 tablespoons HERSHEY'S Cocoa
- 1 tablespoon marshmallow creme
- 2 cups vanilla ice cream

In blender container place milk, peanut butter, cocoa and marshmallow creme. Cover; blend. Add ice cream. Cover; blend until smooth. Serve immediately.

About three 6-ounce servings

Spiced Mocha (from mix)

Chocolate Egg Nog

4 cups milk, divided
4 eggs, separated
1/3 cup HERSHEY'S Cocoa
1 can (14 ounces) sweetened
    condensed milk
1 teaspoon vanilla extract
1/4 teaspoon salt
2 teaspoons brandy extract*
1 teaspoon rum extract*
    Grated chocolate

In blender container combine 1 cup milk, egg yolks, cocoa, sweetened condensed milk, vanilla and salt. Cover and blend on high speed until smooth, about 30 seconds. Pour mixture into large mixing bowl; stir in remaining 3 cups milk and extracts, blending well. Beat egg whites until soft peaks form; gently fold into milk mixture. Chill thoroughly. Stir well before serving. Sprinkle with grated chocolate.
About eight 6-ounce servings

*Note: 1/2 cup rum, brandy or bourbon may be substituted for extracts.

hocolate Strawberry Cooler 🟤

- ½ cup sliced strawberries
- 2 tablespoons sugar
- 1 tablespoon HERSHEY'S Cocoa
- 1 cup milk, divided
- ½ cup club soda, freshly opened
- Ice cream or whipped cream
- 2 fresh strawberries (optional)

In blender container combine sliced strawberries, sugar, cocoa and ½ cup milk. Cover; blend until smooth. Add remaining ½ cup milk and club soda; cover and blend. Pour into 2 glasses. Garnish with ice cream or whipped cream and strawberry, if desired. Serve immediately.

About two 8-ounce servings

Cappuccino Cooler 🟤

- 1½ cups cold coffee
- 1½ cups chocolate ice cream
- ¼ cup HERSHEY'S Syrup
- Crushed ice
- Whipped cream

In blender container place coffee, ice cream and syrup. Cover; blend until smooth. Serve immediately over crushed ice. Garnish with whipped cream.

About four 6-ounce servings

Chocolate Strawberry Cooler

Sauces, Toppings & Frostings

Try these delicious sauces, toppings and more with your favorite dessert.

From left to right: Peanut Butter Sauce, Mocha Satin Sauce (recipes page 90) and Bittersweet Chocolate Sauce (recipe page 91)

Peanut Butter

Bittersweet Chocolate

Peanut Butter Sauce ⊛

1 cup REESE'S Peanut Butter
    Chips
1/3 cup milk
1/4 cup whipping cream
1/4 teaspoon vanilla extract

In small saucepan place peanut butter chips, milk and whipping cream. Cook over low heat, stirring constantly, until chips are melted and mixture is smooth. Remove from heat; stir in vanilla. Serve warm. Cover; refrigerate leftover sauce.

About 1 cup sauce

To reheat: Place sauce in small saucepan. Stir constantly over low heat until warm. Add additional milk or whipping cream for desired consistency.

Mocha Satin Sauce

1/2 cup butter
1 cup sugar
1 cup whipping cream
1/3 cup HERSHEY'S Cocoa
1 teaspoon powdered instant
    coffee
1 teaspoon vanilla extract

In small saucepan over low heat melt butter. Stir in sugar, whipping cream and cocoa. Cook over medium heat, stirring frequently, until mixture begins to boil. Reduce heat; simmer 5 minutes. Remove from heat; stir in instant coffee and vanilla. Serve warm or cool. Cover; refrigerate leftover sauce.   *About 2 cups sauce*

To reheat: Place sauce in small saucepan. Stir constantly over low heat until warm.

Fluffy Cocoa Topping ⊛

2 packages (3 ounces each)
    cream cheese, softened
1/3 cup sugar
1/4 cup HERSHEY'S Cocoa
3 tablespoons milk
2 cups frozen non-dairy
    whipped topping, thawed

In small mixer bowl beat cream cheese, sugar and cocoa. Add milk; beat until smooth and fluffy. Stir in whipped topping. Serve as topping for unfrosted cakes.

About 2 1/4 cups topping

One-Bowl Buttercream Frosting ⊛

6 tablespoons butter or
    margarine, softened
HERSHEY'S Cocoa:
    1/3 cup for light flavor
    1/2 cup for medium flavor
    3/4 cup for dark flavor
2 2/3 cups confectioners' sugar
1/3 cup milk
1 teaspoon vanilla extract

In small mixer bowl cream butter. Blend in cocoa and confectioners' sugar alternately with milk; beat to spreading consistency (additional milk may be needed). Blend in vanilla.   *About 2 cups frosting*

Chocolate Lover's Ice Cream Sauce Ⓝ

1/2 cup HERSHEY'S Syrup
30 HERSHEY'S KISSES, unwrapped
Any flavor ice cream

In small heavy saucepan combine syrup and KISSES; stir lightly. Cook over very low heat, stirring constantly, until KISSES are melted and mixture is smooth. Remove from heat. Spoon sauce over ice cream. Serve immediately. Cover; refrigerate leftover sauce.

About 1 cup sauce

To reheat: In large bowl containing about 1 inch very hot water place smaller bowl containing sauce. Allow to stand several minutes to soften; stir to desired consistency.

Microwave Directions: In small microwave-safe bowl combine syrup and KISSES; stir lightly. Microwave at HIGH (100%) 15 seconds; stir. Microwave additional 30 seconds; stir until KISSES are melted and mixture is smooth. If necessary, microwave additional 15 seconds or as needed to melt KISSES.

To reheat: Microwave at HIGH a few seconds at a time until warm.

Bittersweet Chocolate Sauce

2 cups (12-ounce package)
    HERSHEY'S Semi-Sweet
    Chocolate Chips
2 squares (2 ounces)
    HERSHEY'S Unsweetened
    Baking Chocolate,
    chopped
1 cup whipping cream
1 1/2 teaspoons vanilla extract

In top of double boiler over hot, not boiling, water place chocolate chips, baking chocolate and whipping cream. Cook, stirring frequently, until chocolate is melted and mixture is smooth. Remove from heat; stir in vanilla. Serve warm. Cover; refrigerate leftover sauce.

About 2 cups sauce

To reheat: Place sauce in small saucepan. Stir constantly over low heat until warm.

Chocolate Whipped Cream Frosting Ⓒ

2 tablespoons confectioners'
    sugar
1 tablespoon HERSHEY'S
    Cocoa
1 1/2 cups chilled whipping
    cream
1/4 cup HERSHEY'S Syrup

In small mixer bowl stir together confectioners' sugar and cocoa. Stir in whipping cream. Beat until stiff; blend in syrup. Chill until desired consistency.

About 2 1/2 cups frosting

Fudge Frosting

1 cup sugar
1/4 cup HERSHEY'S Cocoa
1/2 cup milk
1/4 cup butter or margarine
2 tablespoons light corn syrup
Dash salt
1 1/2 cups confectioners' sugar
1 teaspoon vanilla extract

In medium saucepan combine sugar and cocoa. Stir in milk, butter, corn syrup and salt. Cook over medium heat, stirring constantly, until mixture comes to a full boil. Boil, stirring occasionally, 3 minutes. Remove from heat; cool to lukewarm. In small mixer bowl place confectioners' sugar; stir in chocolate mixture and vanilla. Beat until spreading consistency.

About 2 cups frosting

Chocolate Peanut Butter Sauce ✪

1/2 cup HERSHEY'S Chocolate Fudge Topping
1/2 cup HERSHEY'S Syrup
1/4 cup creamy peanut butter

In small saucepan place all ingredients. Cook over low heat, stirring constantly, until mixture is warm. Serve immediately over ice cream or other desserts.

About 1 1/4 cups sauce

Mocha Butter Frosting ✪

1 teaspoon powdered instant coffee
1 teaspoon hot water
1/4 cup butter or margarine, softened
3 tablespoons HERSHEY'S Cocoa
1 teaspoon vanilla extract
1 egg, beaten
2 cups confectioners' sugar

In small mixer bowl dissolve instant coffee in water. Blend in butter, cocoa and vanilla. Blend in egg. Gradually beat in confectioners' sugar until well blended. Add water, 1 teaspoon at a time, if necessary, until desired consistency.

About 1 3/4 cups frosting

Jiffy Chocolate Frosting ✪ Ⓝ

1 cup HERSHEY'S Semi-Sweet Chocolate Chips
1 cup confectioners' sugar
1/3 cup evaporated milk

In small microwave-safe bowl place chocolate chips. Microwave at HIGH (100%) 1 minute; stir. Microwave at HIGH additional 30 seconds or until melted and smooth when stirred. Gradually add confectioners' sugar and milk, beating until smooth.

About 1 1/4 cups frosting

Quick Black Forest Fondue

- 2 jars (12 ounces each) maraschino cherries, with stems
- 1 cup HERSHEY'S Milk Chocolate Chips
- 1 cup HERSHEY'S Semi-Sweet Chocolate Chips
- 1 can (5 ounces) evaporated milk
- 1/4 to 1/2 teaspoon almond extract

Drain cherries; set aside. (If desired, cherries may be placed on flat tray in freezer at least 1 hour before serving.) In medium saucepan combine chocolate chips and evaporated milk; stir lightly. Cook over very low heat, stirring constantly, until chocolate is melted and mixture is smooth. Remove from heat; stir in almond extract. Pour into fondue pot or chafing dish; dip cherries into warm fondue.

About 1 1/2 cups fondue

Creamy Chocolate Frosting

- 3 squares (3 ounces) HERSHEY'S Unsweetened Baking Chocolate
- 1 cup miniature marshmallows
- 1/2 cup butter or margarine, softened
- 1/3 cup milk
- 2 1/2 cups confectioners' sugar
- 1/2 teaspoon vanilla extract

In top of double boiler over hot, not boiling, water melt baking chocolate. Add marshmallows; stir frequently until marshmallows are melted. Pour mixture into small mixer bowl. Beat in butter and milk until mixture is smooth. Add confectioners' sugar and vanilla; beat to desired consistency.

About 2 1/2 cups frosting

Sweetened Whipped Cream ☺

- 1 cup chilled whipping cream
- 1 to 2 tablespoons confectioners' sugar
- 1/2 teaspoon vanilla extract

In small mixer bowl combine cream, confectioners' sugar and vanilla; beat until stiff. Serve cold.   *About 2 cups topping*

Spiced Cream ☺

- 1/2 cup chilled whipping cream
- 1 tablespoon confectioners' sugar
- 1/4 teaspoon vanilla extract
- 1/4 teaspoon ground cinnamon Dash ground nutmeg

In small mixer bowl combine all ingredients; beat until stiff.

About 1 cup topping

INDEX

ISBN O-7853-0504-1

Manufactured in U.S.A.

Pictured on the front cover: Chocolatetown Special Cake (*see page 17*).

Microwave cooking times given in this publication are approximate. Numerous variables, such as the microwave oven's rated wattage and startin temperature, shape, amount and depth of the food, can affect cooking time Use the cooking times as a guideline and check doneness before adding more time. Lower wattage ovens may consistently require longer cooking times.

If you have any questions or comments about the recipes in this book, or about any of our fine Hershey products, please write us at The Hershey Kitchens, P.O. Box 815, Hershey, PA 17033-0815, or call us, toll-free, weekdays 9 a.m.–4 p.m. Eastern time, at 1-800-468-1714.

HERSHEY'S®

FABULOUS DESSERTS

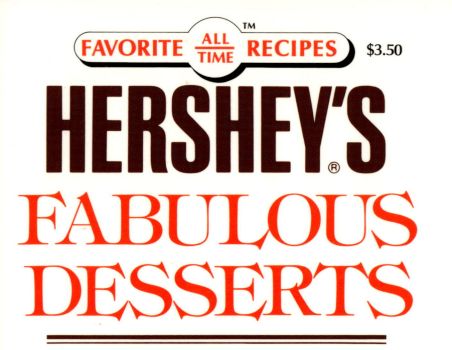